God and Elizabeth Bishop

Santa Efigênia, where slaves worshipped. Elizabeth Bishop's favorite church in Ouro Prêto, Brazil. Photo by Michael Harper. Used by permission.

GOD AND ELIZABETH BISHOP
MEDITATIONS ON RELIGION AND POETRY

Cheryl Walker

"As soon as such [an aesthetic] experience is used to illuminate a life-historical situation and is related to life problems, it enters into a language game which is no longer that of the aesthetic critic. The aesthetic experience then not only renews the interpretation of our needs in whose light we perceive the world. It permeates as well our cognitive significations and our normative expectations and changes the manner in which all these moments refer to one another."

Jurgen Habermas

palgrave
macmillan

GOD AND ELIZABETH BISHOP

© Cheryl Walker, 2005.

First published in 2005 by
PALGRAVE MACMILLAN™
175 Fifth Avenue, New York, N.Y. 10010 and
Houndmills, Basingstoke, Hampshire, England RG21 6XS
Companies and representatives throughout the world.

PALGRAVE MACMILLAN is the global academic imprint of the Palgrave Macmillan division of St. Martin's Press, LLC and of Palgrave Macmillan Ltd. Macmillan® is a registered trademark in the United States, United Kingdom and other countries. Palgrave is a registered trademark in the European Union and other countries.

ISBN 1–4039–6631–1

Library of Congress Cataloging-in-Publication Data is available from the Library of Congress.

A catalogue record for this book is available from the British Library.

Design by Newgen Imaging Systems (P) Ltd., Chennai, India.

First edition: July 2005

10 9 8 7 6 5 4 3 2 1

Printed in the United States of America.

For Butch and Colin
"blessed is he who cometh in the name of the Lord"

Contents

ACKNOWLEDGMENTS

I am deeply grateful to the Bogliasco Foundation for granting me the opportunity to spend a beautiful month in Italy working on this manuscript, to the Earhart Foundation for their generous support of this project during my sabbatical, and to Scripps College for giving me released time, travel grants, financial support, and scholarly recognition. Bishop scholars are a generous lot and it has been my great pleasure to become familiar with many of them. To Bishop scholars Thomas Travisano, Sandra Barry, Camille Roman, Gary Fountain, Brett Millier, and to Butch Henderson, Colin Thompson, and Lacy Rumsey (who are *not* Bishop scholars), I am especially indebted for their contributions to this project. My husband, Michael Harper, traveled with me to Brazil and Nova Scotia, took beautiful photographs, argued with me about the poems, and gave me the benefit of his enormous intelligence. My son, Ian De Heer, provided significant help in the preparation of the manuscript, and my daughter, Louisa De Heer, made life gayer on the darkest days. To everyone who helped and to my students who listened to endless disquisitions on Elizabeth Bishop, I offer my heartfelt thanks.

Permission to reprint work by Elizabeth Bishop has been provided by Farrar, Straus, and Giroux, LLC, as follows: Excerpts from THE COLLECTED PROSE by Elizabeth Bishop. Copyright © 1984 by Alice Helen Methfessel. Excerpts from THE COMPLETE POEMS 1927–1979 by Elizabeth Bishop. Copyright © 1979, 1983 by Alice Helen Methfessel. Excerpt from "After the Rain" from the forthcoming book, EDGAR ALLAN POE AND THE JUKEBOX by Elizabeth Bishop, edited by Alice Quinn. Copyright © 2005 by Alice Helen Methfessel. Excerpts from unpublished letters and unpublished prose written by Elizabeth Bishop. Copyright © 2005 by Alice Helen Methfessel. Reprinted by permission of Farrar, Straus, and Giroux, LLC, on behalf of the Estate of Elizabeth Bishop.

For access to unpublished materials by Elizabeth Bishop, I also wish to thank Special Collections, Vassar College Libraries, and Washington University Libraries Department of Special Collections, St. Louis, Missouri.

Permission to reprint "There's a Certain Slant of Light" is granted by the publishers and the Trustees of Amherst College from THE POEMS OF EMILY DICKINSON, Thomas H. Johnson, ed., Cambridge Mass.: The Belknap Press of Harvard University Press, Copyright © 1951, 1955, 1979, 1983 by the President and Fellows of Harvard College.

The excerpt from "The Drunken Fisherman" is published with the permission of Farrar, Straus, and Giroux, LLC. The excerpt is from COLLECTED POEMS by Robert Lowell. Copyright © 2003 by Harriet Lowell and Sheridan Lowell.

U.S. rights to reprint poems by Marianne Moore granted by Simon and Schuster as follows: Lines from "What Are Years?" reprinted with the permission of Scribner, an imprint of Simon & Schuster Adult Publishing Group, from THE COLLECTED POEMS OF MARIANNE MOORE by Marianne Moore. Copyright © 1941 by Marianne Moore; copyright renewed © 1969 by Marianne Moore. Lines from "In Distrust of Merits" reprinted with the permission of Scribner, an imprint of Simon & Schuster Adult Publishing Group, from THE COLLECTED POEMS OF MARIANNE MOORE by Marianne Moore. Copyright © 1944 by Marianne Moore; copyright renewed © 1972 by Marianne Moore. Lines from "The Jerboa" reprinted with the permission of Scribner, an imprint of Simon & Schuster Adult Publishing Group, from THE COLLECTED POEMS OF MARIANNE MOORE by Marianne Moore. Copyright © 1935 by Marianne Moore; copyright renewed © 1963 by Marianne Moore and T. S. Eliot.

Non-North American rights to republish lines from Marianne Moore's poetry granted by Faber and Faber Limited as follows: from COLLECTED POEMS by Marianne Moore, © 1951. The version of "Luke 14: A Commentary" first appeared in *Cross Currents* and was revised from JOURNEY by Kathleen Norris © 2001. Reprinted by permission of the author and University of Pittsburgh Press. Lines from Rilke from THE SELECTED POETRY OF RAINER MARIA RILKE by Rainer Maria Rilke, translated by Stephen Mitchell, copyright © 1982 by Stephen Mitchell. Used by permission of Random House. Lines from Rumi, translated and reworked into English poetry by Coleman Barks, used by permission of Coleman Barks, Maypop Press, Athens, Georgia, 2004.

U.S. rights to reprint lines from Wallace Stevens' "Sunday Morning" from THE COLLECTED POEMS OF WALLACE STEVENS by Wallace Stevens, copyright © 1954 by Wallace Stevens and renewed 1982 by Holly Stevens. Used by permission of Alfred A. Knopf, a division of Random House, Inc. World (non-U.S. and Canadian) rights to reprint lines from "Sunday Morning" in COLLECTED POEMS by Wallace Stevens, granted by Faber & Faber Ltd. "The Descent" by William Carlos Williams is reprinted from THE COLLECTED POEMS 1939–1962, VOLUME II, copyright © 1948, 1962 by William Carlos Williams. Reprinted by permission of New Directions Publishing Corp.

1

Time and Eternity

Beginnings

Let us begin with recent history, with wars, terrorist acts, plagues, and natural disasters of biblical proportions. In the wake of so much misery, we need to remember, with Walt Whitman, Ralph Waldo Emerson, and William Wordsworth, that eternity lies around us every day. Even those who profess no faith in God have had experiences of it—in love, in nature, and in art. Such experiences, of course, are the lifeblood of poetry, and, though poetry seems forbidding to many, it remains the most memorable form of literary art, furnishing us—faithful and atheist alike—with words to express our most profound feelings.

In the West, the poetry of the Bible is constantly before us in everything from advertisements to political rallies: "For now we see as through a glass darkly, but then face to face"; "To every thing there is a season and a time to every purpose under heaven"; "And now abideth faith, hope, charity, these three; but the greatest of these is charity." The problem with Biblical language, however—and especially the phrases that are most frequently quoted—is that it can so easily sound like cliché. We hardly hear it any longer because we have heard it so often. In *The Perennial Philosophy* (1946), Aldous Huxley put his finger on this problem when he wrote: "Unfortunately, familiarity with traditionally hallowed writings tends to breed, not indeed contempt, but something which, for practical purposes, is almost as bad—namely a kind of reverential insensibility, a stupor of the spirit, an inward deafness to the meaning of the sacred words" (11). To counteract this deafness, he proposed in his book to use less well-known spiritual texts for their great advantage of being "more vivid and, so to say, more audible" than the familiar ones.

Some of Huxley's sources, such as the thirteenth-century Sufi mystic Jalal-uddin Rumi, were not only theologians but also poets of great power, and recently Rumi has enjoyed an unexpected revival, partly because his poetry has been translated into English verse by a gifted poet of our own time, Coleman Barks. Rumi's poems are memorable for their intense sensuality, but often he is playing games with us, inviting us to move beyond our dance to the music of time into something awhirl with eternity. Consider, for example, "Now That I Know How It Is," from Barks's volume entitled *Open Secret* (26), where Rumi writes of the Beloved, here imagined as a character at a love-drunk music festival.

> Who is luckiest in this whole orchestra? The reed.
> Its mouth touches your lips to learn music.
> All reeds, sugarcane especially, think only
> Of this chance. They sway in the canebrakes,
> Free in the many ways they dance.
>
> Without you the instruments would die.
> One sits close beside you. Another takes a long kiss.
> The tambourine begs, *Touch my skin so I can be myself.*
> Let me feel you enter each limb bone by bone,
> That what died last night can be whole today.
>
> Why live some soberer way and feel you ebbing out?
> I won't do it.
> Either give me enough wine or leave me alone,
> Now that I know how it is
> To be with you in a constant conversation.

For Rumi, Time and Eternity carried on a constant conversation, a conversation he entered into with the Beloved, God. It's no wonder that so many of us who are hungry for something beyond the banality of our everyday lives have found Rumi engaging. His books, according to Coleman Barks, sell more copies in America today than those of any other poet.

But there are also wonderfully vivid moments in the works of more modern poets—moments, as in a Rumi poem, that open the receptors of the soul. These may be found even in such unlikely places as in the volumes of skeptical or generally secular individuals, as well as in the works of more self-consciously "spiritual" poets. In this book, I propose to reexamine some traditional Christian concepts such as sin and spiritual love, using the life and poetry of Elizabeth Bishop for inspiration. Bishop was not a practicing Christian herself, but she had been raised both Baptist and Presbyterian, was fascinated with religious ideas, and was often nostalgic for a time in which God was more spiritually present. Though her poetry (like all good poetry) is rooted in actual experience, it reaches beyond anecdote to something less temporal and more profound. Might we call it "eternity"?

In her life, too, Bishop was often aware of the double-edged sword of time. The notes she took during her fateful first trip to Brazil make this especially clear:

> This trip is a "shake-down" trip for me, all right. I know I am feeling, thinking, looking, sleeping, dreaming, eating & drinking better than in a long long time, & when I read something like "The question about time is how change is related to the changeless"—& look around—it doesn't seem so hard or far off. The nearer clouds seem to be moving quite rapidly; those in back of them are motionless—Watching the ship's wake we seem to be going fast, but watching the sky or the horizon, we are just living here with the engines pulsing, forever. (Quoted in Millier, 239)

Time, timelessness, and the shifting perspectives that bring each into focus: these were topics that Elizabeth Bishop often pondered.

ELIZABETH BISHOP: AN UNCONVENTIONAL LIFE

Lives unfold in time, but like poetry they sometimes stammer. From a certain point of view, life can seem to be "just one damn thing after another." But from another viewpoint, such as that of clinical psychology, experiences may surface again and again in a person's life, creating the appearance of a pattern. In the case of Elizabeth Bishop one can easily find patterns of obsessive repetition. There were also typical intellectual predilections and turns of phrase that, among other things, made her literary voice recognizable. Yet, despite these signature gestures, there is always more to say, and in Bishop's case one must be wary of settling too quickly on any one angle or summary of her character. As she herself was fond of saying: *it all depends*.

One thing that is often said about Bishop is that she was skeptical and no doubt in many moods she was. Furthermore, she made some rather severe criticisms of Christians (as dogmatic, judgmental, and condescending). But this is certainly not all there is to say about her relationship to faith, which I will argue was considerably more complicated than has been acknowledged. Because she was an intellectual, because she was a woman, because her mother died in a madhouse, because she traveled widely, because she had friends who were practicing Christians, because she had friends who disdained such practices, because she knew the Bible well and read theology all her life, because she was a lesbian but also loved men, because she was an alcoholic, because her spirit was restless and agnostic, because she had a lively sense of humor, because she loved hymns, because she kept wondering, because she wrote poems: because of all these things and many more, faith to her was like a broken tooth that she kept worrying with her tongue. For all these reasons, too, she is nearer to us, to the real dilemmas of our times, than many a more conventional believer. The story of Elizabeth Bishop's life, like all life stories, can be told in many ways. One can emphasize the stammer, the way she kept stumbling over the same things again and again, or one can emphasize the pattern of her development, the growth of her mind in maturity. Both accounts are "true" and both are relevant to any discussion of time and eternity as they play out not only in her experiences of life but also in her poetry. Here, in this "unconventional" version of her life, I want to pay special attention to matters of religion. The fact that this was not the *main* focus of her life means that this version of her life will be shorter. Shorter need not mean less interesting, however. It all depends, in this case, upon you, "the reader."

Disorder and Early Sorrow

To begin with, Bishop did not have an easy childhood, though to say this is not to say much. (How many of us did, after all?) But Bishop's childhood was *unusually* vexed by disorder and early sorrow. Her father died suddenly before she was a year old. Then her mother's mental health disintegrated virtually before the child's eyes. It did not happen all at once, of course, but it did seem to happen in spectacularly awful (and memorable) "scenes." First her mother went into mourning and severe depression. Then there were the disruptions of normalcy that children feel so keenly: her mother in and out of mental hospitals, Elizabeth repeatedly displaced from Worcester, Massachusetts (where she was born in 1911), to Boston, where her mother was sometimes "in care," to Great Village, Nova Scotia, where her maternal grandparents lived. It was her grandparents who provided the little stability Elizabeth was to know for many years.

Bishop later recorded some of her memories of her traumatic early life in both prose and poetry. In 1914 she and her mother were in Marblehead, Massachusetts, during the Salem fire and, though the mother does not seem particularly unstable in the memories Bishop records in her unpublished poem "A Drunkard," the child feels that her parent is stern and unreachable. The thirst from which the child suffers in her crib goes unrelieved, though others, no more needy or deserving, are being given refreshments. When she picks up a woman's black cotton stocking, discarded in the aftermath of the fire, her mother tells her to "Put that down!" Bishop recounts the story thus

> I picked up a woman's long black cotton
> stocking. Curiosity. My mother said sharply
> Put that down! I remember clearly, clearly—
> But since that day, that reprimand
> that night that day that reprimand—
> I have suffered from abnormal thirst—
> I swear it's true and by the age
> of twenty or twenty-one I had begun
> to drink, and drink—I can't get enough
> and, as you might have noticed,
> I'm half drunk now . . . . (Quoted in Colwell, 235–36)

Clearly, her mother's emotional inaccessibility was deeply wounding, and even as an adult Bishop stammers when she remembers "that day, that reprimand." Once they moved to Nova Scotia, the child Elizabeth seems to have given up hope of a return to normalcy. In Bishop's later harrowing account of her mother's descent into madness, called "In the Village," she distances herself from her mother in various ways, one of which is through control of the narrative. One senses how carefully she represents herself as a child who is doing everything she can so as not to be engulfed by emotion. Bishop writes: "First, she [her mother] had come home, with her child. Then she had gone away again, alone, and left the child. Then she had come home. Then she had gone away again, with her sister; and now she was home again" (*The Collected Prose*, hereafter *CPr*, 252). She "had not got any better," in spite of the trips, in spite of the doctors, and now the child lives on tenterhooks. What will happen?

What happens is "a scream." Or at least that is what might be called the "objective correlative" or psychological substitute that Bishop chooses to encompass the moment of breakdown, the moment the child has been fearing and waiting for. Though the scream is not the end of the story (other events succeed it), it is from another point of view the unending truth of the story, the eternity of loss exposed in that moment of time. Though it is in a profound sense "the end," Bishop begins her story with it:

> A scream, the echo of a scream, hangs over that Nova Scotian village. No one hears it; it hangs there forever, a slight stain on those pure blue skies, skies that travelers compare to those of Switzerland, too dark, too blue, so that they seem to keep on darkening a little more around the horizon—or is it around the rims of the eyes?—the color of the cloud

of bloom on the elm trees, the violet on the fields of oats; something darkening over the woods and waters as well as the sky. The scream hangs like that, unheard, in memory—in the past, in the present, and those years between. It was not even loud to begin with, perhaps. It just came there to live, forever—not loud, just alive forever. Its pitch would be the pitch of my village. Flick the lightning rod on top of the church steeple with your fingernail and you will hear it. (*CPr*, 251)

What is striking about this passage, at first, is the way trauma casts her in the role of an observer, forever cataloging features of the natural world, "the color of the cloud of bloom on the elm trees," for instance. When she was older, Bishop would often quote Rimbaud's image of eternity as "the sea gone off with the sun" (Rimbaud, 139), noting how it delighted her. The image is peculiar (not very resonant to me), but perhaps it conveyed to her mind something special, something that "came there to live, forever," the loss of *both* her parents, her mother the sea (*mater, mare*) and her father the sun/son, conventional enough associations to a literary mind. In her mind, it seems, these events were inextricably tied to observable aspects of the natural world.

What is strange to us today is that once her mother was institutionalized for the last time (in Dartmouth, Nova Scotia), she *never saw her again.* Elizabeth was five years old when her mother went in and twenty-three when her mother died there eighteen years later. Gertrude Bulmer Bishop was declared incurably insane and, though her parents and sisters sent presents, faithfully delivered weekly by young Elizabeth to the village postmaster, they did not suggest a visit. When Elizabeth grew old enough to visit on her own, she shrank from the ordeal that had been successfully postponed for so many years. According to Frank Bidart, however, she lived to regret her procrastination. "Oh, I should have gone to see her" (Fountain and Brazeau, 5), he remembers her saying, descending as she frequently did into self-recrimination.

How does religion play into all this? Why is the scream preserved on the tip of the Presbyterian church steeple, for example, a steeple described elsewhere in the story as "in the middle of the view, like one hand of a clock pointing straight up"? Does the church (like the scream) stop time? Or does it redeem it? Why is it, in addition to Bishop's insistence on observation and accuracy, "in the middle of the view"?

In some ways Bishop saw religion as offering comfort. In a high school story that she wrote about her life with her grandparents during her mother's decline, she says: "We became quite stolidly a family when he [Grandfather] read the Bible" (Millier, 7). On the other hand, "In the Village" associates religion in many ways with what is terrifying and alien rather than what is familiar and reassuring.

The scream occurs during a dressmaker's visit, when her mother is having a new dress fitted, a purple dress that will mark an end to four years of mourning. Somehow Bible stories get confused with the new dress in the child's mind: "Drummers sometimes came around selling gilded red or green books, unlovely books, filled with bright new illustrations of the Bible stories. The people in the pictures wore clothes like the purple dress, or like the way it looked then" (*CPr*, 252). The dressmaker looks like the Old Testament's King Nebuchadnezzar eating grass as she crawls around on her knees with straight pins in her mouth. The mother has preserved some postcards once sent to her, postcards with little hard *crystals* on them in different colors. "Some cards, instead of lines around the buildings, have words written in their skies with the *same stuff*, crumbling, dazzling and crumbling, raining down a little on little people who sometimes stand about below: pictures of Pentecost?" (255). Not a very uplifting image of Pentecost, if so. These *crystals* are like the perdurable essence of the tears that the desolate grandmother cries in secret for her deteriorating daughter (further represented in the poem "Sestina"). The child is dying to get away from the unhappy house and go out with the cow to pasture. But when she makes her escape, a terrifying "Mr. Chisholm" waylays her on the hill, demanding to know how her soul is doing. He holds her hands tightly while he says a prayer and then she "felt a soul, heavy in my chest, all the way home" (265). The church is described as "high-shouldered and secretive" (261). It seems as though the whole universe, a universe presided over by "God," has been infected by the mother's scream. Even when she is gone, perhaps especially when she is gone, the scream with its portent of irremediable suffering casts a shadow over everything. It floats up at the end of the story, into that dark, "too dark," blue sky and becomes one with the elements: "earth, air, fire, water."

In the aftermath of her mother's breakdown and institutionalization, Elizabeth went on living with her grandparents, clinging to the world of this village, which was so full of meanings both comforting and terrifying. Her sense of security had been deeply shaken, but like all children she tried to make sense of things and thus to alter them.

Until I was teased out of it, I used to ask Grandmother, when I said goodbye, to promise me not to die before I came home. A year earlier I had privately asked other relatives if they thought my grandmother could go to heaven [though she had] a glass eye. (Years later I found out that one of my aunts had asked the same question when she'd been my age.) Betsy was also included in this deep but intermittent concern with the hereafter; I was told that of course she'd go to heaven, she was such a good little dog, and not to worry. Wasn't our minister awfully fond of her, and hadn't she even surprised us by trotting right into church one summer Sunday, when the doors were open? (*CPr*, 6–7)

By this time Elizabeth needs this reassurance because she is clearly having doubts about the justice and reasonableness of God. And when her tall, imperious paternal grandfather swoops down and dislodges her from her Great Village home (an event she remembers as a virtual kidnapping), he is not surprisingly described as "god-like," gods apparently being those who are allowed to be capricious without apology.

Any child might wonder about a God who would inflict such pain for no apparent reason on the "little people who sometimes stand about below," like herself and her plain but devout Canadian grandparents. But even later in life, Elizabeth Bishop seemed at times to carry a special grudge against religion that cannot be entirely explained by these early experiences of suffering. There was anger—mixed, it seems, with a kind of panic—that would suddenly resurface at particularly difficult times in her life.

We can see this anger in the story called "The Baptism" that Bishop wrote shortly after the death of her mother in 1934. The story takes place in a country village much like the Great Village of Bishop's childhood, where indeed some of the events it recounts actually occurred (baptisms in icy water, subsequent deaths). Three orphaned sisters struggle to stave off poverty ("How would they get through the winter?") but they find ways to survive by mutual support and self-discipline. The church is an important feature of their lives. "They were Presbyterians. The village was divided into two camps, armed with Bibles: Baptists and Presbyterians. The sisters had friends on both sides" (*CPr*, 161).

Life and death are often intermixed in this rural environment. A neighbor drops in to say that her sister's baby has died, "although they had done everything. She and Emma, Flora, and Lucy [the three sisters] discussed infant damnation at some length. Then they discussed the care of begonias, and Mrs. Peppard took home a slip of theirs" (161).

The story grows darker when Lucy, who is not yet a church member, decides to join the Baptists instead of the Presbyterians as her sisters have done. As the plot unfolds, Lucy becomes increasingly possessed by her religious crisis, which will be resolved, she feels, only when she can experience baptism by total immersion. "She felt very guilty about something" (163). Lucy punishes herself by not eating, cries frequently, and even sees God. He is found sitting on the stove. "God, God sat on the kitchen stove and glowed, burned, filling all the kitchen with a delicious heat and a scent of grease and sweetness." The fire imagery suggests that this god is in fact a devil: " 'His feet are in hell,' she remarked to her sisters" (167), in an aside worthy of Flannery O'Connor.

When Lucy insists on her baptism in the icy river still surrounded by snow banks and then becomes delirious with fever, she claims to see God again, so it's no surprise when we are told that she died the next night. But Bishop ends the story ironically, refusing to give us a place to locate our anger: "The day she was buried was the first pleasant day in April, and the village turned out very well, in spite of the fact that the roads were deep with mud. Jed Leighton gave a beautiful plant he had had sent from the city, a mass of white blooms. Everyone else had cut all their geraniums, red, white, and pink" (170). THE END. Something is uncomfortably awry here, however, and its traces may be seen in that odd phrase "the village turned out very well." What can that mean?

As we can see from this story, the specter of religious fanaticism haunted Elizabeth Bishop and made her particularly unsympathetic to those who imposed their religious beliefs on others. Certain forms of religious belief seemed to her like violations, as when Mr. Chisholm grabs the child taking the cow to pasture and inflicts upon her the unwanted pressure of his faith. By another kind of person or a person with a different history, these peculiar gestures might have been shrugged off as merely unpleasant accidents, but in "The Baptism" Bishop comes close to suggesting that religion is downright dangerous for the fragile, the innocent, and the unwary. They cannot be comforted by the strange statement that "the village turned out very well" and neither can we as readers. Lucy, in the throes of religious fanaticism, did not turn out very well and that is what the reader will probably feel is most important; that horror is what is foreshadowed by the conversation about "infant damnation," a particularly unpalatable concept.

Bishop herself, of course, was one of those innocents at risk when her mother's mental health gave way (her baptism by fire), and it is significant that religious imagery becomes enmeshed in the child's memories of her deterioration: the purple dress, for example, that reminds her of the Biblical illustrations in the "unlovely" books sold by door-to-door salesmen. But why the panic? Why equate religion with madness?

Gary Fountain's oral biography of Bishop provides a telling hint that might help to answer this question. Grace Bulmer, Gertrude's sister and Elizabeth's favorite aunt, mentions that Bishop's mother grew increasingly fanatical about religion as she became more and more deranged. She suffered from terrible feelings of guilt, resulting in fantasies of being burnt as a witch, hanged, or electrocuted. Her peculiar hypersensitivity reminds one of Bishop's, and of Lucy's in "The Baptism": "She felt very guilty about something."

An even more suggestive moment occurs in Bishop's poem called "The Moose" where the narrator reports overhearing the conversations of elderly people on a Greyhound bus. They are like "Grandparents' voices / uninterruptedly / talking, in Eternity" (The Complete Poems, hereafter *CP*, 171). They tell stories about "deaths, deaths and sicknesses" and one set of these is the following:

> He took to drink. Yes.
> She went to the bad.
> When Amos began to pray
> even in the store and
> finally the family had
> to put him away . . . (172)

Perhaps it is not too outlandish to suggest that these folks represent Bishop and her mother, transformed in the poem and thus to some extent redeemed, if only by the colloquialism of living memory. Elizabeth "took to drink." Since her mother, here called "Amos," had spells of religious mania, perhaps her incarceration was connected in Elizabeth's mind to this. Then it would not be surprising if Bishop, in a fit of what Freud calls "displacement," became both angered and frightened by those who were too fervently evangelical about their religious beliefs. This might also explain why Bishop never became a "believer," though she was in many ways attracted to the ideas of faith.

The great twentieth-century substitute for religion, psychoanalysis, she regarded with a similar mixture of attraction and repulsion, writing in 1942 to her friend Marianne Moore about Karen Horney's book *The Neurotic Personality of Our Time*: "I had infinitely rather approach such things from the Christian view, myself—the trouble is I've never been able to find the books, except [George] Herbert" (Merrin, 40).

This, however, was more than a little disinguous, because she found books on virtually every other subject and could, if she had wished, have located something of interest to connect God with the psyche. Jeredith Merrin comments that "her personal losses are persistently bound up with a sense of vanished orthodox Christian belief" (42). She found Christian sermonizing repellent, but throughout her life she could never quite turn her back on that special world of increased significance, spiritual striving, and renewal that religion at its best inhabits. That's why Merrin insists that Bishop's poetry is "permeated by religious nostalgia, and haunted by what she called the 'old correspondences' " (9).

Youth, Friends, Books, and Ideas

Instead of religion, Elizabeth Bishop found poetry and in the process found Marianne Moore, a mother-mentor who combined a settled religious faith with an experimental poetic edge. The librarian at Vassar College, where Bishop was a student, introduced them; they arranged to meet at the New York Public Library, and they quickly developed a great liking for one another. Moore was considerably older, an eccentric given to odd costumes such as her famous three-cornered hat, but she had a quirky and wonderful wit. Bishop wrote of her: "She must have been one of the world's greatest talkers: entertaining, enlightening, fascinating, and memorable; her talk, like her poetry, was quite different from anyone else's" (*CPr*, 124). Furthermore, she had already published a great deal, whereas Bishop was then just a schoolgirl who had published a few things in minor publications. The relationship was not romantic but it was intensely rewarding because they soon discovered they had a lot in common: a fascination with plants and animals, a rarefied taste in literary matters ("priceless vocabularies" as Bishop noted in her poetic tribute to Moore), an attraction to the exotic, but also certain fundamental values. In "Efforts of Affection: A Memoir of Marianne Moore," Bishop speculates that the letter M, Moore's monogram, came to mean "mother; manners; morals" to her. Though she teased Marianne a little about her fastidiousness, and smiled at a certain prudishness that made her object to words such as "water-closet" in a poem, Bishop admired Moore's delicacy, honesty, probity, and industriousness, virtues her own mother had not possessed. To Bishop, Moore had a "Protestant, Presbyterian, Scotch-Irish" literalness to her, something valuable left over from the Puritans.

About religion they agreed to disagree. "We never talked about Presbyterianism, or religion in general, nor did I ever dare more than tease her a little when she occasionally said she believed there was something *in* astrology" (*CPr*, 155). Since Marianne lived with her mother, however, Mrs. Moore was often a solemn and devout third party at their encounters, and sometimes Mrs. Moore repeated the gesture of the dreaded Mr. Chisholm, grabbing Elizabeth's hand and saying a prayer over her as Bishop left the apartment. "She wrote me one or two beautifully composed little notes on the subject of religion, and I know my failure to respond made her sad" (*CPr*, 129). Yet Bishop had great affection for Mrs. Moore, admiring the precision and balance of her language, and the occasional ironic remark, as when Mrs. Moore agreed about the new turn Marianne's work was taking: "Yes. I am so *glad* that Marianne has *decided* to give the inhabitants of the *zoo* . . . a *rest*" (*CPr*, 129). (Moore, of course, was known for her many poems about exotic animals.)

In many ways, the two Moores (mère and fille) seemed miraculously suited to remind Bishop of her past and to usher in her future. They were "old-fashioned" people, "but even more, otherworldly—as if one were living in a diving bell from a different world, let down through the crass atmosphere of the twentieth century. Leaving the diving bell with one's nickel [for the subway], . . . one was apt to have a slight case of mental or moral bends" (137), Bishop wrote.

Despite her anachronistic traits, however, Marianne Moore was also, in another realm, an avant garde Modernist. She was admired by T. S. Eliot and published in the ultramodern magazine *The Dial*. If discussions of religion were off limits, discussions of poetry could in many respects make up for them. Both Elizabeth and Marianne liked seventeenth-century religious poetry, especially George Herbert's. Both knew by heart many poems by the early-twentieth-century Jesuit poet Gerard Manley Hopkins.

In fact, Moore was one of the few to recognize Bishop's poetry as being religious in its depths, commenting in her review of *North and South*, "Miss Bishop's speculation also, concerning faith—religious faith—is a carefully plumbed depth" (Schwartz and Estess, 179). For her part, Marianne's poetry, which Bishop learned to greatly admire, could be quite theological as well. "In Distrust of Merits," for example, written during the Second World War, is a serious attempt to approach the issue of war from a Christian perspective. Bishop praised it, and for good reason. This was a form of self-accusation—holding oneself to account before accusing others of wrongdoing—that, unlike her mother's pathological sense of guilt, Bishop could respect. The poem is a valuable counterbalance to the kind of narcissistic passions excited by armed conflict. It ends:

> . . . . "When a man is prey to anger,
> he is moved by outside things; when he holds

his ground in patience patience
patience, this is action or
beauty," the soldier's defense
and hardest armor for
the fight. The world's an orphan's home. Shall
we never have peace without sorrow?
without pleas of the dying for
help that won't come? O
quiet form upon the dust, I cannot
look and yet I must. If these great patient
dyings—all these agonies
and wound bearings and bloodshed—
can teach us how to live, these
dyings were not wasted.
Hate-hardened heart, O heart of iron,
iron is iron till it rust.
There never was a war that was
not inward; I must
fight till I have conquered in myself what
causes war, but I would not believe it.
I inwardly did nothing.
O Iscariot-like crime!
Beauty is everlasting
and dust is for a time. (137–38)

Time and eternity. Here they play out differently from the way they did in Bishop's story of her childhood "In the Village." Eternity is not endless and irremediable loss but "action or beauty" manifest in the world, something that echoes the goodness of God. And time, though full of suffering, is always passing away, becoming something else. Eternity experienced within time can be fullness, even superfluity, as well as embargo. And, as Bishop recognizes in some of her poems, the soul assents to it, even when the experience of it is transient. The ending of Moore's "What Are Years?" puts it this way:

satisfaction is a lowly
thing, how pure a thing is joy.
This is mortality,
this is eternity. (95)

In "What Are Years," mortality (time) and eternity become one, at least for a precious, precarious moment.

In addition to Marianne Moore, there were others who helped Bishop to nourish her spiritual appetite without committing her to a particular dogma. One of the earliest of these was Wallace Stevens, the Hartford insurance executive who wrote so powerfully about the relationship of the world of the senses to the world of ideas. Asked by Ashley Brown in 1966 about early influences, Bishop acknowledged: "I think that Wallace Stevens was the contemporary who most affected my writing then" (Monteiro, 23), and elsewhere she admitted that she had practically memorized Stevens's *Harmonium*.

Stevens, like Bishop, was suspicious of the Church but powerfully moved by beauty, especially that to be found in nature. In "Sunday Morning," one of Stevens's most famous poems and one that specifically rejects organized religion in favor of a pagan devotion to nature, we find a woman reflecting on her sense of the limits of Christianity.

> Why should she give her bounty to the dead?
> What is divinity if it can come
> Only in silent shadows and in dreams?
> Shall she not find in comforts of the sun,
> In pungent fruit and bright, green wings, or else
> In any balm or beauty of the earth,
> Things to be cherished like the thought of heaven?
> Divinity must live within herself:
> Passions of rain, or moods in falling snow;
> Grievings in loneliness, or unsubdued
> Elations when the forest blooms; gusty
> Emotions on wet roads on autumn nights;
> All pleasures and all pains, remembering
> The bough of summer and the winter branch.
> These are the measures destined for her soul. (5)

Despite the lovely sound of the words, one might well pause at the rather narcissistic treatment of nature in this woman's thoughts: "gusty / emotions on wet roads on autumn nights." Yet in many ways they mirror Stevens's own thoughts. David Jarraway quotes an early letter by Stevens that reads: "An old argument with me is that the true religious force in the world is not the church but the world itself: the mysterious callings of Nature and our responses. What incessant murmurs fill that ever-laboring, tireless church!" (22).

Stevens was not a Christian in any conventional sense, but he believed that the major poetic idea is and has always been the idea of God, and thus he can help us to see why poets of great talent and ambition so often find themselves in the realm of religion even when they do not see themselves as bound by a religious faith. A Modernist and, to some degree, a skeptic, Stevens nevertheless wrote: "While it can lie in the temperament of very few of us to write poetry in order to find God, it is probably the purpose of each of us to write poetry to find the good which, in the Platonic sense, is synonymous with God" (Jarraway, 2). Even more reminiscent of Bishop's own views, of her religious nostalgia and sense of loss, is Stevens's statement that "My trouble, and the trouble of a great many people, is the loss of belief in the sort of God in Whom we were all brought up to believe" (2). However, Stevens much more than Bishop went through *stages* of belief and disillusionment. ("Sunday Morning" was written in one of the early stages.) Guy Rotella finds Stevens eventually losing his faith (in God, in nature, in the imagination), but holding on to a kind of meaning nevertheless, generated by the repeated urge to resist the onslaught of meaninglessness. "Like curtains in the house of the metaphysician," Rotella writes, "our need for knowledge fills and fails and swells. In our 'old chaos of the sun' [a phrase from 'Sunday Morning'], the absence of absolutes lays us low and lifts us up" (140). These words might well apply to Elizabeth Bishop as well.

In 1973, six years before her death, Bishop was finishing a semester of teaching at Harvard before doing a brief stint at the University of Washington. Her course on modern poetry addressed the work of Wallace Stevens (as well as Robert Lowell, e. e. cummings, William Carlos Williams, and Marianne Moore). It is interesting that her final exam for the course asks the students to identify parts of poems by each author, all of which "have two large themes in common: the conditions of mortality, and the possibility, or impossibility of immortality" (Vassar Archive). Her Stevens extract (from "To An Old Philosopher in Rome") juxtaposes time and eternity: in Rome "Two parallels become one, a perspective, of which / Men are part both in the inch and in the mile." The world of the flesh and the world of the spirit, time and eternity: these are issues that concerned both Wallace Stevens and Elizabeth Bishop all their lives.

Since, unlike Stevens, Bishop did not go through a series of stages in her thinking about such matters, she was always, in a sense, vacillating. What one can say with certainty is that poetry gave her access to realms of feeling and states of consciousness that she associated not just with the body but also with the soul. Helen Vendler recalls that Bishop insisted that real poets have to write, no matter what else is going on in their lives. "She further explained that writing would take authority over being busy or whatever because if you didn't write you immediately would feel it by your condition of body or soul" (Fountain and Brazeau, 300–01).

Many years earlier, in 1934, she had explained her view of the way poetry mediates between time and eternity in a journal entry:

It's a question of using the poet's proper material, with which he's [*sic*] equipped by nature, i.e., immediate, intense physical reactions, a sense of metaphor and decoration in everything—to express something not of them—something, I suppose, *spiritual*. But it proceeds from the material, the material eaten out with acid, pulled down from underneath, made to perform and always kept in order, in its place. Sometimes it cannot be made to indicate its spiritual goal clearly (some of Hopkins', say, where the point seems to be missing) but even then the spiritual must be felt . . . . This is why genuine religious poetry seems to be about as far as poetry can go—and as good as it can be. (Quoted in Merrin, 57–58)

In the Key West Notebook (hereafter KWN) from the 1930s, she copied out a quotation from Kierkegaard: "Poetry is illusion before knowledge; religion illusion after knowledge. Between poetry and religion the worldly wisdom of living plays its comedy. Every individual who does not live either poetically or religiously is a fool" (41, Vassar Archive).

The idea that there is something fundamentally spiritual about the highest forms of poetry (and of life) was a notion that she shared (at least during the first years of their relationship) with Robert Lowell. Though Lowell was younger by several years, he was already a seasoned poet when they first met in 1947. They connected immediately and no doubt had much in common. Lowell's marriage to Jean Stafford had broken up partly because of his manic engagement with Roman Catholicism. Though she did not share his views, Bishop, in contrast to Stafford, found Lowell's religious bent not unattractive. Both had been deeply moved by the religious poetry of Gerard Manley Hopkins. Joseph Summers remembers a poetry conference in 1948, attended by Bishop, where Lowell was in his element: "Listening to Lowell talk about the gospel of St. John in very literary-religious terms was wonderful. He and Elizabeth seemed to be very much in love that weekend" (Fountain and Brazeau, 106).

Although Bishop admitted to several people that she was strongly attracted to Lowell, even in love with him, she held off from expressing her feelings because she knew that Lowell was mentally unstable and represented aspects of herself and her past that she found frightening. Lowell, for his part, lavished praise on Bishop's work, dedicated poems to her, and even confessed that he had always expected to marry her, but somehow it never happened. Blessedly, instead of a love affair, their relationship turned into a lifelong friendship punctuated by visits and letters.

As Lowell's poetry moved away from religion toward family and history, Bishop continued to admire it. Yet the historical aspect of Lowell's poetic imagination was something Bishop did not really share. In "Brazil, January 1, 1502" she attempted a Lowellian perspective on the past (Lowell loved the poem), but fundamentally she was a geographer of the spirit. "More delicate than the historians' are the map makers' colors," she had once concluded in her early poem "The Map."

While their relationship developed, through hundreds of letters written across several decades, Lowell and Bishop rarely discussed religion, but there seemed to be an understanding between them that when deeper movements of the heart and mind occurred, they might share them with one another. Thus, in 1955, Lowell, having lapsed from Catholicism some years earlier, wrote to Bishop in Brazil: "I shouldn't say this I suppose—about two months ago after much irresolution I became an Episcopalian again (a high one). I used to think one had to be a Catholic or nothing. I guess I've rather rudely expected life to be a matter of harsh clear alternatives. I don't know what to say of my new faith; on the surface I feel eccentric, antiquarian, a superstitious, sceptical fussy old woman, but down under I feel something that makes sober sense and lets my eyes open" (unpublished letter, L53 May 5, 1955).

On May 20 Bishop responded:

I am glad you told me about the Episcopalian Church. I have no right to speak about things I know so little about—but it seems to me the best things of the Christian tradition lie with it at present, maybe, rather than in the Catholic Church—and here [in Brazil], particularly, one feels more and more disgusted with the Catholic Church I'm afraid.— Although a couple of my best and brightest friends are very Catholic, and of course everyone is by education, I wish I had the 39 articles on hand. I also wish I could go back to being a Baptist!—not that I ever was one—but I believe now that complete agnosticism and straddling the fence on everything is my natural posture—although I wish it weren't. (B71 unpublished)

To be of two minds was characteristic of Elizabeth Bishop. She could never quite relinquish the *desire* to believe, though a settled faith eluded her. In 1954, only a year earlier, she had written an appreciative letter to Joseph Summers about his book on George Herbert, praising Summers's willingness to address "all these insoluble and endless and nagging problems of man's relationship to

God." The problem of faith might seem a bit old-fashioned, but, she insisted: "It is *real*.—It was real and it has kept on being real and it always will be, and Herbert just happened to be a person who managed to put a great deal of it into magnificent poetry,—it is still real for all of us, after all" (unpublished, to Joseph Summers, October 4 or 5, 1954; Vassar Archive).

Though Lowell moved on to other modes, Bishop remained haunted by the notion that "genuine religious poetry seems about as far as poetry can go—and as good as it can be." So in 1973, when she made up that exam for her modern poetry class, it was to Lowell's early *religious* poetry that she returned. "The Drunken Fisherman" with its elevated diction and overtones of rage obviously still captured for her the white heat of the poetic imagination, fusing spiritual passion with brilliant technique.

No doubt this poem also had considerable personal significance for Bishop. It addressed the problems with alcohol that she and Lowell shared. By 1973 Bishop was feeling past her prime in several important ways. Now she, like the drunken fisherman who is speaking in this poem, had to confront the loss of earlier power, and even if she did not end up where he does here, she knew whereof he spoke. Even today, this terrifying monologue—by a speaker consumed by self-loathing—gives me the chills:

> Now the hot river, ebbing, hauls
> Its bloody waters into holes;
> A grain of sand inside my shoe
> Mimics the moon that might undo
> Man and Creation too; remorse,
> Stinking, has puddled up its source;
> Here tantrums thrash to a whale's rage.
> This is the pot-hole of old age.
>
> Is there no way to cast my hook
> Out of this dynamited brook?
> The Fisher's sons must cast about
> When shallow waters peter out.
> I will catch Christ with a greased worm,
> And when the Prince of Darkness stalks
> My bloodstream to its Stygian term . . .
> On water the Man-Fisher walks. (37–38)

Did Elizabeth Bishop also wish to "catch Christ with a greased worm"? She denied it, claiming in a letter to Anne Stevenson in 1964:

> You are probably right about a "sense of loss" [in my poems] and it is probably obvious where it comes from [childhood?]—it is not

religious. I have never been religious in any formal way and I am not a believer. I dislike the didacticism, not to say condescension, of the practicing Christians I know (but maybe I've had bad luck). They usually seem more or less on the way to being fascists. But I am interested in *religions*. I enjoy reading, say, St. Theresa [*sic*], very much, and Kierkegaard (whom I read in vast quantities long ago, before he was fashionable), Simone Weil, etc.—but as far as people go, I prefer Chekov. (Unpublished letter)

Here Bishop may be seen as quarreling more with the practice of religion than with religion itself (note the reference to fascism, which, as Camille Roman has shown, was deeply distressing to her but no more so than communism or indeed any enforced system of belief that, from her point of view, did not allow for reasoned dissent). On the score of religion, though, one sometimes feels that she doth protest too much. Though she was an outspoken opponent of overblown pieties, her reading carried her into areas that are generally not of much interest to the truly secular person. This is true of such texts as St. Ignatius's *Spiritual Exercises*, an intensely Christo-centric text that involves minute instructions concerning religious meditation. She read it in the early 1930s, well before it became popular among literary critics, and used it as a poetic resource many times. No one could be less accommodating to the skeptical reader than Ignatius. Here is a typical passage concerning the third prelude to the first day of contemplation, which is to be dedicated to the incarnation: "*The third prelude* will be to ask for what I desire. Here it will be to ask for an interior knowledge of our Lord, who became human for me, that I may love him more intensely and follow him more closely" (148). And so it goes—"day by day"—for 200 pages. St. Teresa's *Way of Perfection*, which Bishop kept with her in all climes, is also intensely preoccupied with the minutiae of religious life. Those not seriously interested in what Emily Dickinson called "the flood subject" might dabble in such readings, but it is hard to imagine that they would subject themselves to such a difficult and demanding course of meditational study.

Furthermore, though Bishop denied that she had a "mythology," Christianity furnished her with a whole host of images and ideas. At one time she expected to write a book on the story of Tobias and the Angel, from the Book of Tobit. Her letters and journals are peppered with references to Job, Jonah, St. Sebastian, and other Biblical characters, and she actually did write a wonderful poem on the Prodigal Son. In 1951 she told Robert Lowell about a new book of poems to be called "Concordance," after her long poem on the Bible called "Over 2,000 Illustrations and a Complete Concordance." She exulted, "I had my doubts [about 'Concordance' for the title] but yesterday morning, just as I was leaving the hotel in Halifax, I picked up the Gideon Bible and thought I'd make one of those test samplings, you know. My finger came right down on the concordance column, so I felt immensely pleased" (*One Art*, 223).

Bishop's literary correspondent Flannery O'Connor wrote many stories about people who are convinced that they are not believers but stumble into God on their way somewhere else. In O'Connor's world people are stalked by the Lord, who inevitably gets them in the end, since the unconscious, for O'Connor, always seems to harbor the Holy Ghost, and the Hound of Heaven is relentless. Though Bishop never quite reached the point of turning at bay, shortly before her death she was reading Augustine's *City of God*. It, too, is not "an easy read," though many passages are poetic to some degree, such as the following:

> It is, therefore, because we are men [human], created to the image of a Creator, whose eternity is true, his Truth eternal, his Love both eternal and true, a Creator who is the eternal, true, and lovable Trinity in whom there is neither confusion nor division, that, wherever we turn among the things which He created and conserved so wonderfully, we discover his footprints, whether lightly or plainly impressed. (Book XI, ch. 28, 239)

Bishop might well have responded simply to the stammering language of this passage but her real concern, at this stage of her life, was with death and the possibility of immortality. To that end she was eager to find a description of the City of God with its promise of peace. Augustine says, "peace is so universally loved that its very name [pax] falls sweetly on the ear" (Book XIX, ch. 11, 451). In Augustine's rendering of the City of God, there is no necessary conflict between time and eternity, the City of Man and the City of God. They exist simultaneously until death intervenes and one falls away:

> The City of God, however, has a peace of its own, namely, peace with God in this world by faith and in the world to come by vision . . . . But in that final peace which is the end and purpose of all virtue here on earth, our nature, made whole by immortality and incorruption, will have no vices and experience no rebellion from within or without. There will be no need for reason to govern non-existent evil inclinations. God will hold sway over man, the soul over the body; and the happiness in eternal life and law will make obedience sweet and easy.

And in each and all of us this condition will be everlasting, and we shall
know it to be so. (Book XIX, ch. 27, 480–81)

This is the kind of passage, near the end, that might have appealed
to the troubled spirit of Elizabeth Bishop. Peggy Ellsberg remembers
Bishop's agitation in June of 1979—Bishop died in October—and in
the oral biography, she recalls:

> When I got there, she [Elizabeth] was somewhat agitated. She was
> reading *The City of God* by Saint Augustine, and she was near the end.
> She said, "I want to believe this. It is one of the most exciting things
> I've ever read. I called you because I know you are a Catholic
> and I want to hear what you have to say." I can't remember what I said.
> I remember her taking one of my hands in both of her hands [uncon-
> sciously imitating Mr. Chisholm and Mrs. Moore?] and saying: "If only
> I had a daughter, if only I'd had a child, I wouldn't feel so bad now."
> That was the last time I saw her. The subject that day was immortality
> and everlasting life and life after death. I remember saying to her,
> "I have no child, but I have no doubts about immortality." She said,
> "That's why I called you." (Fountain and Brazeau, 347–48).

In Prison

Through most of her life Bishop remained a prisoner of her body. She
suffered from severe asthma, eczema, bronchitis, and other nervous
ailments; these were allergies that seemed to have been triggered initially by her removal from Great Village and "incarceration," as she
saw it, in the house of her paternal grandparents in Massachusetts.
"The combination of severe illnesses that struck her in Worcester—
acute asthma, eczema, and even symptoms of St. Vitus' dance—almost
killed her in that first winter with her paternal grandparents," according
to Marilyn May Lombardi (51).

In her short story about this experience, significantly called "The
Country Mouse," Bishop dramatizes the profound dismay she felt
owing to this violent displacement. After her unpretentious Bulmer
grandparents in Canada, the wealthy Bishops seemed cold and aloof,
given more to objects than to people. Yet as Bishop tells the story of
being a "country mouse" suddenly transplanted to a more urbane but
also more threatening city environment, she makes it funny. She even
criticizes her younger self for trying to get a new friend (Emma) to
feel sorry for her by saying that her mother has died instead of admitting
that she is alive but in a mental institution. The only member of the
household with whom Elizabeth completely identifies seems to be

the dog Beppo, about whom she tells a humorous story:

> There was a dog, a Boston bull terrier nominally belonging to Aunt Jenny, and oddly named Beppo. At first I was afraid of him, but he immediately adopted me, perhaps as being on the same terms in the house as himself, and we became very attached. He was a clever dog; he wore a wide collar with brass studs, which was taken off every night before he went to bed. Every morning at eight o'clock he would come to my door with the collar in his mouth, and bang it against the door, meaning for us to get up and dressed and start the day together. Like most Boston terriers he had a delicate stomach; he vomited frequently. He jumped nervously at imaginary dangers, and barked another high hysterical bark. His hyperthyroid eyes glistened, and begged for sympathy and understanding. When he was "bad," he was punished by being put in a large closet off the sewing room and left there, out of things, for half an hour. Once when I was playing with him, he disappeared and would not answer my calls. Finally he was found, seated gloomily by himself in the closet, facing the wall. He was punishing *himself*. We later found a smallish puddle of vomit in the conservatory. No one had ever before punished him for his attacks of gastritis, naturally; it was all his own idea, his peculiar Bostonian sense of guilt. (*CPr*, 21)

It *is* a funny story except for the fact that, for Bishop too, guilt over negligible offenses got all tangled up with the body and some not quite articulated sense of metaphysics, as though simply being human and embodied might mean one had to take responsibility for the misery of the world. At the end of this story, seven-year-old Elizabeth has an experience of what might almost be described as existential nausea. While waiting for her aunt at the dentist's, she looks at the three others in the waiting room and feels not just unnecessary (what the French call "*de trop*") but worse than that: implicated in a fallen world of isolation, embodiment, and error. The story ends on a strange note:

> I felt, *I, I, I*, and looked at the three strangers in panic. I was *one* of them, too, inside my scabby body and wheezing lungs. "You're in for it now," something said. How had I got tricked into such a false position? I would be like that woman opposite who smiled at me so falsely every once in a while. The awful sensation passed, then it came back again. "You are you," something said. "How strange you are, inside looking out. You are not Beppo, or the chestnut tree, or Emma, you are *you* and you are going to be *you* forever." It was like coasting downhill, this thought, only much worse, and it quickly smashed into a tree. *Why* was I a human being? (*CPr*, 33)

Crime and punishment. Like Beppo, Elizabeth here seems overly fastidious, blaming herself for things she cannot help, imagining a voice (God's?) threatening her with punishment for some transgression ("You're in for it now"), and then even imagining it coming to pass when her thought smashes into a tree. "The feeling of self-distaste" (32) that overcomes her when she lies to Emma about her mother becomes generalized here into a broader sense of panic. Clearly, we are dealing with a person of acute, even neurotic, sensibilités. One explanation for allergic reactions is that they are triggered the first time by repressed feelings of hostility that generate guilt. According to this theory, the body is taking revenge upon itself. Furthermore, as we now know, stress robs the immune system of its ability to combat disease, so any severe psychological distress puts one in physical jeopardy. In Bishop's writing there is plenty of evidence of guilt, but one wonders to what extent she was aware of the nature of her guilty feelings. How did they attach her to, or detach her from, religion, and how did they affect her writing?

We can only speculate about such matters but it certainly seems that the metaphysical traditions of Protestantism were firmly embedded in Bishop's unconscious. No matter what she said about her conscious beliefs, conceptions of the Fall, in which we are born into sin and guilt, persisted. In fact, one might speculate that it was precisely in order to avoid confronting her own sense of fallenness that Bishop insisted upon *not knowing* certain things. She resisted psychotherapy, for example, though she was as fascinated with her dreams as any Freudian and kept track of them, one might almost say, religiously.

In her essay "The Closet of Breath: Elizabeth Bishop, Her Body and Her Art," Marilyn May Lombardi helpfully reminds us that Bishop felt it was important for the artist *not* to understand everything she was doing. "Poetry should have more of the unconscious spots left in," she wrote in one of her Key West Notebooks. "What I tire of quickly in Wallace Stevens is the self-consciousness—poetry so aware lacks depth" (Lombardi, 58).

Though much has been written about Bishop's psychology, especially as it related to her sexuality, religion was also an area of life that inspired complex feelings, not all of which were consistent with one another. The body and its longings were often tainted in her mind with feelings of guilt even while, at another level, Bishop felt martyred by her physical disabilities and angered by the suggestion that they were somehow *merely* psychosomatic.

Of course, there is nothing pleasant about suffering that is simultaneously mental and physical. And there is no doubt that Bishop suffered the pangs of hell trying to cope with her asthma, which often put her in the hospital. On her first trip to Brazil, she had a violent allergic reaction to the fruit of the cashew, which almost killed her. Lombardi tells the story this way.

Taking fifteen cubic centimeters of calcium and seven or eight cubic centimeters of adrenalin each day to bring her swelling down, Bishop was suffering simultaneously from a "very bad" recurrence of her childhood eczema, an inflammatory condition of the skin characterized by oozing lesions that become scaly, crusted, or hardened . . . . With the worst case of eczema since childhood, her "ears swollen like large red hot mushrooms," and her asthma as bad as ever, Bishop wrote to [her doctor at home] with frustration and a hint of justifiable self-pity: "I finally got sick of being stuck with so many things [to reduce the swelling, and felt] like St. Sebastian." (Quoted in Lombardi, 48)

But the (here humorous) sense of being a martyr could quickly dissolve into a darker sense of culpability or at least of shame. Like St. Teresa she felt that complaining about one's infirmities was a form of self-indulgence. In *The Way of Perfection*, Bishop's favorite book by the Spanish nun, the point insisted upon repeatedly is humility. Teresa says, "Try not to fear these [afflictions] and commit yourself wholly to God, come what may. What does it matter if we die? How many times have our bodies not mocked us? Should we not occasionally mock them [laugh at them] in our turn?" (96). In her letters Bishop *did* mock her afflictions, and it is easy to imagine her relishing St. Teresa's no nonsense approach. But her life was, nonetheless, deeply and adversely affected by these problems with her health.

Bishop was also tormented by another health problem, her dependence upon alcohol. In some moods she explained her addiction genetically, as an inheritance from her family, several of whom, she claimed, were alcoholics. But then again she was liable to feel that she herself was at fault. An excruciating sense of guilt emerges in some of her letters to her doctor, Anny Baumann, to whom she was not always completely truthful. In one she writes: "OF COURSE I know I shouldn't drink, and I try hard not to. I have missed only one class in five years [not true] because of this and I have NEVER taken a drink before class . . . . I feel I can't bear to be made to feel guilty *one more time* about the drinking. There *are* things that are worse, I think, and I hope you can help me with them" (quoted in Millier, 506).

There were times in Bishop's life when she was drunk for days, when she scoured the house for any alcoholic substance and drank whatever she found, including eau de cologne, becoming horribly sick in the process. Carley Dawson remembers letting Bishop stay in her apartment in Washington, D.C.:

I had a little house that I was renting on O Street and asked Elizabeth if she would like to stay there. I didn't know that she was a lush, and under the stairs was a cupboard where I had an assortment of liquor. It never occurred to me to put them away. I left the house in charge of my maid and a friend to keep an eye on her. When I came back, they said that she had taken a little of everything and the vomit on everything all over the house was something to behold. They cleaned it all up. I said something to Elizabeth about it, like "What had happened about the liquor?" And she said, "I got feeling sorry for myself one night and I started tasting all the different things. I just started, couldn't stop." (Fountain and Brazeau, 109–10)

There were numerous episodes of binge drinking in Bishop's life, but at times she could drink socially without excess or ill effects. Much depended upon her state of mind. It is also true that Bishop used drinking as a way of gaining access to emotions and memories that she couldn't bring to consciousness otherwise. At certain periods of her life, when she was deeply (or as she put it, "hysterically") unhappy, she felt the sense of time break down: "the past & the present seemed confused, or contradicting each other violently and constantly, & the past wouldn't 'lie down' . . . . this was really taught to me by getting drunk, when the same thing happens, for perhaps the same reasons, for a few hours" (Millier, 224).

Veering wildly between self-pity and self-disgust, Bishop was drawn to a passage in the work of W. H. Auden that she copied out and under-scored with a reminder to herself: "DO NOT FORGET this FIRST QUOTE . . . MOST IMPORTANT OF ALL." The first quote was the following:

The drunk is unlovely to look at, intolerable to listen to, [and] his self-pity is contemptible. Nevertheless, as not merely a worldly failure, but also a [willful] failure, he is a disturbing image for the sober [citizen]. His refusal to accept the realities of this world, babyish as it may be, compels us to take another look at this world and reflect upon our motives for accepting it. (As quoted in Millier, 384)

The curious justification that comes at the end provides an inkling of the way alcohol figured in the life of Bishop and indeed in the lives of many artists: as personal failure but also as defiant critique.

Strangely enough, the inebriate is not so different from the mystic (which is why Rumi uses the metaphor of drunkenness to speak of spiritual ecstasy in "Now That I Know How It Is," quoted earlier). There are many kinds of intoxication, including those of the true believer and the masochist, who may share parts of the same psychological terrain. Bishop came close to inhabiting the mind of the masochist (a position well known to people who suffer with painful incurable illness) when she wrote her marvelous story "In Prison," in which she makes interesting connections among the artist, the religionist, and the incarcerated.

The story begins, in a very Kafka-esque manner, in the voice of the narrator: "I can scarcely wait for the day of my imprisonment. It is then that my life, my real life, will begin. . . . The reader, or my friends, particularly those who happen to be familiar with my way of life, may protest that for me any actual imprisonment is unnecessary, since I already live, in relationship to society, very much as if I were in a prison. This I cannot deny, but I must simply point out the philosophic difference that exists between Choice and Necessity" (*CPr*, 181). This is a narrator who *demands* necessity, possibly because choice is too threatening.

The prison seems to be an alternative to the asylum, which in some ways it resembles. But the narrator says: "I do not feel that what is suited to an asylum is necessarily suited to a prison. That is, because I expect to go to prison in full possession of my 'faculties'—in fact, it is not until I am securely installed there that I expect fully to realize them—I feel that something a little less rustic, a little harsher, might be of more use to me personally" (186–87).

One cannot help but feel a certain theological resonance in all of this, as though we are listening to a sinner who longs for the day of his judgment. The narrator casually admits that he has dreamed of Hell and that Hell looked like a prison. And near the end, he volunteers: "You may say—people have said to me—you would have been happy in the more flourishing days of the religious order, and that, I imagine, is close to the truth" (191).

What is the relationship of Elizabeth Bishop to her creation of this peculiar character, one might wonder. Though the narrator is clearly a persona, this is a character who resembles a certain aspect of Bishop's psyche—"the guilty one"—the one who felt she needed the choke chain. Furthermore, this man is not far from certain Christian mystics of the medieval period, such as Julian of Norwich or Catherine of Siena, who were known to engage in acts of self-defilement (eating pus from the wounds of the dying, for instance) as a way of seeking purification and connection to God. Like them, the narrator of "In Prison" wants to be exalted (to gain "authority"), and he too seeks exaltation by way of self-abasement and confinement.

Though Bishop wrote this story many years before she read Simone Weil, "In Prison" is eerily reminiscent of some parts of the French mystic's writing. Bishop was fascinated by Weil, in part because she had "found Christ"—that is, experienced Him as physically present to her—while reciting George Herbert's poem "Love III," which begins, "Love bade me welcome yet my soul drew back." Any poet might well be moved by such a story, but Bishop, as we know, connected religion and poetry more firmly than some poets. Though Bishop claimed that Weil's mysticism was repellent to her, she herself had written a first-person narrative in high school called "Into the Mountain," where her main character (the autobiographical Lucius) has a vision of the Holy Family and eventually stumbles toward "the falls" behind what seems to be an avenging angel. The aura of danger surrounding the supernatural is again unmistakable.

Simone Weil also connected danger with the religious life. She insisted upon putting herself through harrowing physical experiences, including self-starvation, in order to share the plight of the least fortunate, a project she felt brought her closer to Christ. She longed to undertake a suicidal mission during the Second World War and went so far as writing letters soliciting an assignment. In the so-called "terrible prayer" she expressed a longing to be totally deprived of sensory enjoyment: "Father, in the name of Christ, grant me this," it begins, "[t]hat I might be beyond any condition to make any movement of my body, even any hint of movement, obey any of my wishes, like a total paralytic" (quoted in Dargan, 42).

Similarly, in *Waiting for God* she writes, "The most beautiful life possible has always seemed to me to be one where everything is determined, either by the pressure of circumstances or by impulses such as I have just mentioned and where there is never any room for choice." And again: "I always believed and hoped that one day Fate would force upon me the condition of a vagabond and a beggar which [St. Francis] embraced freely. Actually I felt the same way about prison" (63, 65). Like the narrator of "In Prison," she gloried in necessity, even writing a poem in praise of it.

Bishop was neither a mystic nor a masochist, and she hated what she called "spiritual bombast," but at the level of the unconscious, where her imagination found its deepest nourishment, she thought of herself as a creature in need of grace, and when those feelings of unworthiness came to the surface, she could sometimes sound like a soul in purgatory, seeking salvation through acts of contrition. Bishop acknowledged her affiliation with Simone Weil when she wrote to Marianne Moore in 1953: "I'm also reading Simone Weil after staving it off for several years—the mysticism often repels—and then suddenly she says something so amazing & so simple you wonder why no one ever said it before" (*One Art*, 257).

Love and Death

One of the most obvious reasons for the sense of guilt that was mixed up with Bishop's relationship to her body was her lesbianism. Homosexuality was recognized in the 1920s and 1930s, especially among artists and writers, but it was still stigmatized by the general public, and Bishop was hypersensitive to criticism, often internalizing it. She makes gentle fun of Marianne Moore's naiveté concerning such matters but one wonders how Moore's disapproval affected Elizabeth herself. In "Efforts of Affection," written in the far more liberal 1970s, Bishop recounts: "I remember [Marianne] worrying about the fate of a mutual friend whose sexual tastes had always seemed quite obvious to me. 'What are we going to do about X . . . ? Why, sometimes I think he may even be in the clutches of a *sodomite* . . . !' " Bishop comments sardonically, "One could almost smell the brimstone" (*CPr*, 130).

But how funny did it feel to her at the time? One might note as well the connection between religion and moral judgment in the anecdote. If Bishop repeatedly cast Christians in the role of moral policemen, perhaps it was because she had felt the sting of Christianity's traditional prohibition against homosexuality.

Bishop herself was extremely private about her proclivities, insisting that there were benefits to closets. Indeed she said she preferred "closets, closets, and more closets" at a time when gay people were beginning to insist that everyone "come out." Of course, Bishop had many openly gay friends, especially in the latter part of her life, but she herself took pains to conceal the nature of her relationships. Even her love poetry was careful in that respect. Though they are gradually being published now, the more obviously lesbian erotic poems were never meant for general distribution.

However, Margaret Dickie claims: "As a poet, Bishop played with concealment, not just to keep secret her lesbianism and her alcoholism, but because it allowed her to hide—behind masks and complicated structures—a range of emotions and sympathies she did not want to acknowledge fully" (7). That range is precisely what is lost in some readings of Bishop's work, especially those that insist on Bishop as always and forever an ironic observer. Clearly, Elizabeth Bishop had a highly complex temperament, full of contradictions—emotional, intellectual, and spiritual. Like the imaginary iceberg she describes in her poem by that name, she cut her facets from within.

> This iceberg cuts its facets from within.
> Like jewelry from a grave
> it saves itself perpetually and adorns
> only itself, perhaps the snows
> which so surprise us lying on the sea.
> Good-bye, we say, good-bye, the ship steers off
> where waves give in to one another's waves
> and clouds run in a warmer sky.
> Icebergs behoove the soul
> (both being self-made from elements least visible)
> to see them so: fleshed, fair, erected indivisible. (*CP*, 4)

Here the iceberg is compared to the soul ("both being self-made from elements least visible"), but the iceberg is self-sufficient and austere, making us long to see its invisible elements "fleshed, fair, erected indivisible." The poem begins: "We'd rather have the iceberg than the ship, / Though it meant the end of travel." Unlike the human form, it is not vulnerable to the predations of time and death: "it saves itself perpetually" in a sublime form: the word made flesh, the Platonic ideal of a poem, perhaps—infinitely inaccessible but infinitely attractive. Anne Stevenson comments, "The iceberg behooves our souls because it is self-made and pure, godlike, incorruptible, not of human making" ("The Iceberg and the Ship," 56).

In contrast, Bishop's life kept confronting her with the seemingly inevitable conjunction between love and death. Sometimes it is hard to imagine how she could cope with all the deaths and losses she had to absorb, beginning, of course, with her father's death and her mother's deathlike disappearance. She later wrote about the deaths of Cousin Arthur ("First Death in Nova Scotia") and her friend "Gwendolyn," both of which occurred during Bishop's childhood.

Probably more traumatic for her, in terms of early losses, however, was the death of Robert Seaver, because it seemed so clearly calculated to inspire guilt. Seaver, a brilliant young man who had suffered from polio as a teenager and went about on crutches, was Bishop's first serious "beau." According to all accounts he was deeply in love with her. Both in their early twenties, they did spend off-season weekends together on the Cape, but it must have been clear to her by 1936 that she really didn't want to marry him (or any man). So she went off to Europe with her women friends while, despite the fact that he had other female admirers, he moped around at home waiting for news. In the fall Bishop came back, taking up residence in New York; by that time Seaver must have realized that he had lost her. For whatever complicated reasons using whatever convoluted logic, in November he committed suicide. But not before posting her a card that she received a few days after his death, which simply said: "Elizabeth, Go to hell."

Bishop never quite got over the shock of this death and even forty years later she would insist—in drunken moments—that she had ruined Bob Seaver (among others she had loved). Brett Millier comments: "Elizabeth often said that she was 'born guilty'—and this is very likely true. The child of a dysfunctional mother often assumes the burden of responsibility herself, and a guilty self-hatred is also the emotional territory of the alcoholic. A nature as restrained, even as repressed, as Elizabeth's expresses little emotion except under extraordinary circumstances. In this crisis, as in others in her life, alcohol allowed her the expression" (505).

During the 1930s and early 1940s, Bishop had a series of unsuccessful love relationships with several women and possibly one man (Tom Wanning). Neither Louise Crane nor Margaret Miller, both persons of interest during this period, was quite ready to offer Bishop the kind of relationship she wanted. And then there was the horrifying automobile accident in France when Margaret's arm was severed between the wrist and the elbow and Elizabeth had to sit in an open field with her and the severed arm, waiting for assistance. In an episode virtually tailor-made for someone like Bishop, a priest came by to say that the accident was predictable owing to the fact that there had been no man to drive the car. (Was he commenting on the sinfulness of this lesbian ménage—Elizabeth and her lover Louise Crane plus Margaret—or just being sexist?)

In February 1948 Bishop noted that she was "thirty-seven / and far from heaven," but things were about to change. After a stint as Poetry Consultant to the Library of Congress (during which she made dutiful visits to Ezra Pound at nearby St. Elizabeth's), Bishop decided that she had better try traveling again, often her preferred method of distraction. After a brief trip to Sable Island, Canada, she was informed that she had won the Amy Lowell Travel Fellowship, and so in November of 1951 she set out on a freighter bound for South America.

The terrible allergic reaction to the fruit of the cashew that landed her in the hospital also inspired an outpouring of affectionate concern from people she knew in Rio de Janeiro. One of these, Lota de Macedo Soares, became first her nurse and then her lover. Lota was a sophisticated, Europeanized Brazilian from an aristocratic family; she owned property in Rio and was building a home in Petrópolis, several hours north of the city in the mountains. Strong-willed and determined, Lota decided to make Elizabeth an offer she could not refuse. Moved by Bishop's loneliness and her lack of stability and financial resources, she suggested that, if Elizabeth stayed in Brazil, Lota would build her a study at "Samambaia" overlooking a waterfall where she could work without interruptions and without financial worries. Bishop said yes.

Thus began the happiest ten years of her life. In a long letter to Robert Lowell, she explained her new situation in an understated way: "I arrived to visit Lota just at the point where she really wanted someone to stay with her in the new house she was building. We'd known each other well in New York but I hadn't seen her for five or six years. [Neither of these statements was quite true.] She wanted me to stay: she offered to build me a studio—picture enclosed—I certainly didn't really want to wander around the world in a drunken haze for the rest of my life—so it's all fine & dandy." But to her doctor, Anny Baumann, she was far less guarded: "I still feel that I must have died and gone to heaven without deserving to, but I am getting a little more used to it" (both quoted in Millier, 251).

Elizabeth and Lota shared many intellectual interests, not least of which were literature (Bishop's specialty) and architecture (Lota's). Like Bishop, Lota knew several languages, including Portuguese, English, and French, so they could read together, socialize with one another's friends, and travel about comfortably. Both women had strong opinions about the arts, though Lota was more outspoken whereas Elizabeth often kept her views to herself unless she knew the person very well. Both had had other women lovers; in fact, Mary Morse (called Morsey), whom Lota had taken up at an earlier point, also lived on her property and did not seem to mind the new arrangement. Both Lota and Elizabeth were cosmopolitan intellectuals and religious skeptics, though Lota argued with those among her friends who had become "churchy," whereas Elizabeth tended to stay out of such arguments. She was more likely to be fascinated by "true believers," probably because they touched something in her she could never quite grasp.

If one can speak about role-playing in the relationship, it seems that Lota played the more aggressive part and Elizabeth performed the more nurturing role. Elizabeth was more reactive, less combative, and a great cook. Both women loved babies, but Elizabeth seems to have been more "maternal" in her relationship to them. Furthermore, as the following poem suggests, she enjoyed ministering to Lota's needs. In "The Shampoo" this takes the form of washing her lover's hair, which was black with streaks of gray in it. As lovely and intimate as this poem is, it was not immediately accepted for publication, as though editors in the 1950s couldn't quite grasp the situation that inspired it. It was finally published in *The New Republic* in 1955 after rejections by *The New Yorker* and *Poetry*, both of which had published other poems by Bishop.

The still explosions on the rocks,
the lichens, grow
by spreading, gray, concentric shocks.
They have arranged
to meet the rings around the moon, although
within our memories they have not changed.

And since the heavens will attend
as long on us,
you've been, dear friend,
precipitate and pragmatical;
and look what happens. For Time is
nothing if not amenable.

The shooting stars in your black hair
in bright formation
are flocking where,
so straight, so soon?
—Come, let me wash it in this big tin basin,
battered and shiny like the moon. (*CP*, 84)

Years later Bishop recalled a summer night when "Lota woke me up in the middle of the night to go out and look at the stars because they had never looked so *close* before—close and warm, apparently touching our hair—and never so many" (quoted in Millier, 248). The poem, like this memory which it in some way recalls, says much about their relationship, their coming together at this time in their lives, both a bit battered but, at least for a while, luminous with love.

In "The Shampoo" time and eternity are reconciled for a moment when Bishop compares the growth of the lichens (whose constant change goes unnoticed because of daily contact) to "us," who are similarly held in observation by "the heavens." Bishop pokes gentle fun at Lota for being "precipitate and pragmatical" in demonstrating the passage of time so overtly in her gray-streaked hair. She has rushed too soon to exhibit aging and "Time is nothing if not amenable": it is happy to have its power be known. Anne Colwell comments:

> The truth that the lover ages and will die in time, the truth and dread of loss, counterbalances the desire for and rejoicing in connection. In earlier drafts of the poem, then entitled "Gray Hairs," Bishop exhorts the lichens to stay and not to rush to their destination. . . . For Bishop, preserving connection over time, preserving love, involved bargaining with the forces of the universe. In her notes for the third draft of "The Shampoo," she writes "Eternity could always wait of course" (Vassar Archive, Box 29), as though all eternity were what two humans bargained with to achieve their moment of connection. (92–93)

Like many people in the embrace of love, Bishop here suggests that the Beloved links her to something beyond the earth, though their love is not immune to time's passage.

Elizabeth Bishop and Lota de Macedo Soares had many happy years together. Bishop drank less and worked more. But in the end their relationship began to fall apart as Lota became embroiled in Brazilian politics and Elizabeth returned to her destructive drinking. Lota, who had many political connections, was appointed to design and build a multi-use public park for the shoreline of Rio de Janeiro. Though very much the kind of project Lota enjoyed, it was a massive and highly politicized undertaking. In the end it became an unbearable strain on both of them. To get away for a while, Bishop accepted a teaching post (her first) at the University of Washington, but this certainly did not ease the tensions between the two women, as Bishop (whose damaged psyche was incapable of self-sufficiency) became dependent on a much younger woman who had that combination of vitality and efficiency that Bishop always looked for in a partner and indeed needed to survive. She returned to Brazil after the semester ended but carried on a covert correspondence with her new friend, a correspondence that Lota eventually intercepted.

Thus began a hellish time in Elizabeth's life (1966–1967) when her previously stable world completely lost its center. Lota had been under a terrible strain owing to the park, and now *her* mental health began to deteriorate. She was repeatedly hospitalized for anxiety and depression and even given insulin shock treatments. Elizabeth was still deeply devoted to Lota but she could barely stand to be around her. Eventually, at the suggestion of Lota's psychiatrist, a person Elizabeth had also consulted and trusted, they agreed to a separation. Bishop went to New York in the spring and Lota stayed behind in Rio. But no sooner had she gone than Lota found herself miserable and lonely. In September, while still emotionally fragile, she insisted upon coming to New York for a visit. After a pleasant and relatively unproblematic day at Elizabeth's apartment, she took an overdose of pills in the middle of the night and collapsed. She was rushed to St. Vincent's Hospital, where, for a few days, there seemed to be some hope. But after a week, Anny Baumann brought the news that Lota had died, surely reconfirming in Bishop's mind the deep connection in her life between love and death. As with her mother, Elizabeth had not been able to bring herself to visit the comatose Lota in the hospital. And, as with Tom Seaver's death, Bishop felt that she was in some way responsible.

Hilary Bradt remembers: "When I stayed with Elizabeth in Brazil [in 1970], we talked a lot, and she kept reliving Lota's death. It was something very traumatic and profound in Elizabeth's life. Elizabeth was wracked with guilt. She said that Lota fixed her with this awful accusing look after she had taken the pills. Elizabeth was standing at the bottom of stairs and Lota then collapsed. Elizabeth felt there was this great accusation just before Lota died" (Fountain and Brazeau, 233). In Lota's will, Elizabeth discovered an ominous quotation from Voltaire: "Si le Bon Dieu existe, il me pardonnera. C'est son métier." [If there *is* a God of love, he will forgive me. That's his job.] Though an unbeliever for most of her life, Lota like Elizabeth seems to have wavered about the existence of God when it came to facing her own death.

Lota died in 1967, but Elizabeth lived on, despite recurrent problems with alcohol and wretched health, for twelve more years. Friends died—Marianne Moore, Robert Lowell, Flannery O'Connor. Suicides—John Berryman's, Randall Jarrell's, Ernest Hemingway's, Sylvia Plath's—seemed to accumulate around her. Brett Millier recounts one episode from 1975: "When Elizabeth heard that Calvin Kentfield, an old friend from the Yaddo [writers' colony] days, had killed himself, she said dryly: 'I do wish people I know would stop committing suicide'" (504). But she herself faced several desperate moments when she had to be saved from attempts to end her life through excessive drinking and consumption of pills. More than once she was rushed to the hospital to have her stomach pumped.

The surprising thing, though, is that Bishop kept writing and actually composed, or at least finished, some of her best poems during those years. *Geography III*, the last book she put together herself, was in many ways her best, and the "new poems" from 1979, added to *The Complete Poems 1927–1979* published after her death, include the wonderful "Santarém" and "Pink Dog," both memorable poems about Brazil. Bishop could never just set aside the past. It would not "lie down" for her. The good thing about this fact, though, is that her emotions and ideas took shape slowly and ultimately achieved the perfectly natural-seeming richness of expression of poems such as "The Moose," "Crusoe in England," "In the Waiting Room," and "One Art."

Though in some ways permanently scarred by her loss, Bishop went on to love again. After the tempestuous relationship ended with the young woman she had met in Seattle (taken up again after Lota's death), she settled in Boston and taught for several years at Harvard. Again she lost control of her drinking, was hospitalized, and needed someone to take care of her. Again she found someone, miraculously, who was not only willing to take care of her but who was young, attractive, efficient, and willing to love her as well. Over certain kinds of people, Elizabeth Bishop exerted a powerful sexual force, a force Bishop knew she possessed and, despite her debilitating shyness, could often deploy successfully.

But age was catching up with her and in many ways she was becoming something of a burden to those closest to her. Prone to falls that left her with broken bones, resistant to advice, melancholy, and alcoholic, Bishop not infrequently called people up at night and begged them to keep her company so that she wouldn't be left alone with her own thoughts. Even Alice Methfessel, her last guardian angel, sometimes had reservations. At one point she was considering accepting a proposal of marriage. In the grip of the terror that she would lose (or was losing) Alice, Bishop wrote one of her most moving poems, the carefully structured villanelle "One Art" (*CP*, 178):

> The art of losing isn't hard to master;
> so many things seem filled with the intent
> to be lost that their loss is no disaster.
>
> Lose something every day. Accept the fluster
> of lost door keys, the hour badly spent.
> The art of losing isn't hard to master.
>
> Then practice losing farther, losing faster:
> places, and names, and where it was you meant
> to travel. None of these will bring disaster.
>
> I lost my mother's watch. And look! my last, or
> next-to-last, of three loved houses went.
> The art of losing isn't hard to master.
>
> I lost two cities, lovely ones. And, vaster,
> some realms I owned, two rivers, a continent.
> I miss them, but it wasn't a disaster.

—Even losing you (the joking voice, a gesture
I love) I shan't have lied. It's evident
the art of losing's not too hard to master
though it may look like (*Write* it!) like disaster.

Though the poem was directly inspired by her relationship with
Alice (as is even clearer in earlier drafts), Lota is certainly a strong
presence in it as well. The houses, the cities, the continent, the rivers,
all conjure up Brazil as well as other places. The poem recapitulates a
lifetime of loss in which Elizabeth once again finds herself trying to
"master disaster" even if only poetically. The last line is the kicker,
however, because it implies that it may not be possible to master
disaster after all if the disaster is linked to love.

Though this poem has inspired a great deal of critical commentary,
what hasn't been adequately noted is the way it invokes spiritual practices, both Buddhist and Catholic, that emphasize the discipline of
loss. Though Bishop has little to say about Buddhism, in St. Teresa's
Way of Perfection and St. Ignatius' *Spiritual Exercises* she studied the
techniques of letting go that are embedded in the Catholic tradition.
Such techniques reemerge in "One Art," which we might say is a
religious poem whose religious context has been obscured. It is a
religious poem without a God to offer grace.

What is the purpose of practicing "the art of losing," another word
for which might be that spiritually freighted term "renunciation," or
perhaps more accurately "relinquishment"? In an earlier draft, the
comparison between spiritual practices and the art of losing is made clear
where Bishop writes: " 'He who loseth his life, etc.—but he who / loses
his love—neever [*sic*], no never never never again' " (see drafts in
Millier, 507–12). In other words, renunciation makes sense in a religious context because "he who loseth his life [in this world] shall
find it [in eternity]." But in the context of earthly love, there is no
compensation for the heart's loss. It remains quite simply a disaster.

Though she had plenty of doubts about God, Bishop was clearly
attracted to that form of self-control that is strengthened by spiritual
practices. In her strange short story "The Sea and the Shore," her
Bishop-like protagonist (an alcoholic beachcomber) studies scraps of
paper for their relevance to his lonely life. On one of these he finds an
extract (Bishop does not identify the source) from the Twentieth
Introductory Explanation of St. Ignatius. She quotes it as follows:
"The Exercitant will benefit all the more, the more he secludes himself from all friends and acquaintances and from all earthly solicitude,
for example by moving from the house in which he dwelt, and taking

another house or room, that there he may abide in all possible privacy . . . [obliterated] he comes to use his natural faculties more freely in diligently searching for that he so much desires" (*CPr*, 175–76; see Ignatius, 127–28).

One might note the idea of renunciation and the particular reference to surrendering the house, both of which also appear in "One Art." In the *Spiritual Exercises* the point of undertaking this discipline is to free up the spiritual faculties for greater contact with God, presumably what the Exercitant "so much desires." In "One Art" the implication seems to be that disciplining one's unruly emotions, especially the debilitating pain of loss, will serve the purposes of Art, of writing. It is all one, the title ("One Art") seems to imply—mastering the disaster of loss, acknowledging the transitoriness of earthly things, and being able to write about this experience of loss successfully. But clearly there is a residual sense of loss in moving from the "so much desired" person to the writing itself.

At a less obvious level, however, we come back to the conjunction between poetry and religion. Being able to write well means opening up the portals of one's imagination, losing the consciousness of one's limited historical self (even the desiring self), and letting God in. Bishop consciously denied that she was religious but when asked by *Poetry Pilot*, a literary newsletter, to choose seven poems with a common theme, she chose seven hymns, including William Cowper's "God Moves in a Mysterious Way": "Deep in unfathomable mines / Of never-failing skill / He treasures up His bright designs, / And works his sovereign will." God is the artist who most successfully practices the art of mastering disaster, according to Cowper, who insists that "Blind unbelief is sure to err, / And scan His work in vain."

"One Art" was published in *Geography III* in December 1976, and reviewers loved it. In the aftermath of its publication, Bishop won a second Guggenheim, though she was still accepting teaching assignments during her grant year, 1978–1979. She completed "Sonnet" that year, a poem that again suggests the need to free the spirit from its imprisonment in the flesh. And, as we know, Bishop took up St. Augustine and the letters of Flannery O'Connor as though to move beyond being "a creature divided," making the "rainbow-bird," the soul, previously caught in the mirror of self, now free to travel "wherever / it feels like, gay!" (see "Sonnet," *CP*, 192). Though thankfully she did not lose Alice after all, Elizabeth Bishop died in October 1979, of a brain aneurysm.

It would be wrong to suggest that Bishop became a "true believer" at the end of her life. And there is no denying that Bishop, at certain moments, was an outspoken critic of Christianity. Richard Wilbur recounts one of these in Gary Fountain and Peter Brazeau's oral biography:

> The only time that I remember Elizabeth being undelectable, being cross with me, was on the day of a party at John Brinnin's house. When we had taken to the out-of-doors and were having drinks and would soon move on to croquet, Elizabeth took me up on it when I mentioned that we had just been to church. She said something like, "Oh dear, you go to church, don't you? Are you a Christian?" I said, "Well, yes, going to church, I am likely to be a Christian." Elizabeth said, "Do you believe all those things? You can't believe all those things." I said, "Like most people I have my days of believing nothing, and I have my days of believing much of it, and some days I believe it all."
>
>   Then Elizabeth began mentioning points of Christian doctrine that she thought it intolerable to believe. She said, "No, no, no. You must be honest about this, Dick. You really don't believe all that stuff. You're just like me. Neither of us has any philosophy. It's all description, no philosophy." At that point Elizabeth shifted to talking about herself and lamenting the fact that she didn't have a philosophic adhesive to pull an individual poem and a group of poems together, but she was really quite aggressive at that point. It surprised me because of her bringing up, [from which she] had many Christian associations, cared about many Christian things, and had got [them] into her poems here and there. I think that was what she was left with, the questions, if not the answers, of a person with a religious temperament. (Fountain and Brazeau, 348–49)

Whether she might still have said such things at the very end of her life, we don't know, but it does seem that toward the end she was less emphatic about her status as an "unbeliever" and more willing to play with God. Certainly "Santarém" (which I will discuss later and which was finished in 1979) is one of her most celebratory spiritual poems with its reconciliation between immanence and transcendence in the "watery, dazzling dialectic" of the Amazon. And "The End of March" opens a literary window for a manifestation of God as "the lion sun," who, in a delightful moment of divine intervention, "perhaps had batted a kite out of the sky to play with."

What Are Years?

For readers who take religion seriously, a writer who ends up with the questions rather than the answers of a person with a religious temperament may be more enticing and ultimately more satisfying than a dogmatic one. The best writing offers a means of grappling with the serious questions of life, and these are the questions such readers pose to God. Even the Bible raises more questions than it answers, and this is surely why serious readers come back to it year after year, generation after generation. Though this is sometimes lost sight of in secular circles, not all Christians are "fundamentalists." According to Patrick Henry, in *The Ironic Christian's Companion*, " 'a Christian way of knowing' is characterized by candor and concreteness, not theological correctness or pious sentiment. It acknowledges, even revels in, what C. S. Lewis calls 'the roughness and density of life' " (11–12).

From some theological perspectives today, God is more interested in making us pay concrete attention to the world around us than in extracting from us a commitment to a set of narrow religious principles. In her notebook, Simone Weil wrote: "Utmost attentiveness is what constitutes the creative faculty in man, and utmost attentiveness is none other than religious" (Dargan, 90). In this vein, one of Patrick Henry's conclusions seems especially appropriate to Elizabeth Bishop, who was widely admired for her close attention to detail and for her accurate eye. At the end of a chapter called "On Paying Attention," he writes: "That God challenges us to use all the skills of explanation we have is for me an article of faith. That we all, repeatedly, even habitually, use our skills of explanation as a way of evading the challenge God presents to us is for me a matter of observation. That attention upsets explanation and thus deepens, broadens, and enriches life, afflicting us when we are comfortable and comforting us when we are afflicted, is for me a matter of experience" (104–05). In the struggle between "description" and "philosophy" that Richard Wilbur remembers as Bishop's, careful description may, therefore, be the more truly religious option.

In this vision of doing God's will, we can and should direct our attention not only to what is immediately present to our senses but also to the past in its many guises. Elizabeth Bishop's life, as part of that past, remains of interest, it seems to me, because it continues to demonstrate the tensions experienced by many of our most intelligent and reflective contemporaries, especially those associated with the arts. Looking at this life in some detail provides what anthropologists call a "thick description" (that is, a layered and multiperspectival representation) of the factors that impinged upon the consciousness of Elizabeth Bishop the writer and Elizabeth Bishop the thinker, both of whom emerge as compelling figures.

However, if asked whether we should limit ourselves to reading the poems in terms of Bishop's life, I think the answer must be "no."

Bishop herself acknowledged that poems mean far more than the poet consciously intends, and because that is the case, we can and do have access to their language without needing to limit ourselves to considerations of "what she had in mind" during the moments of composition. Bishop herself wrote to Anne Stevenson, "I believe that everyone has the right to interpret [my poems] exactly as he [or she] sees fit" (Stevenson, Elizabeth Bishop, hereafter *EB*, vi). When Stevenson suggested to Bishop in a letter that "A Miracle for Breakfast" must have something to do with the Eucharist, Bishop readily agreed, though she said the thought hadn't occurred to her until a friend translated the poem into Portuguese and said the same thing. Still, in a recent essay entitled "The Iceberg and the Ship," Stevenson argues that Bishop's poetry is, in fact, transcendentalist in its "epiphanic showings forth" (54), and there is much to be said for this position.

It is quite possible to give a religious reading to a text that wasn't written to make a religious point as long as one doesn't do violence to the conventions of informed reading, which are based primarily on the connotative and denotative possibilities of language. Despite what some younger readers want to argue, poems *cannot* mean anything one wants them to mean, but that doesn't imply that they have to mean one thing and one thing only. The possibilities for interpretation are endless because all texts (like all language) possess a surplus of meanings, carrying within themselves more possibilities than any one reader can attend to. As one writer puts it, "Metaphor economizes the surplus" (Detweiler, 40).

In an interesting recent work of literary criticism, *Breaking the Fall: Religious Readings of Contemporary Fiction*, Robert Detweiler argues that religious reading need not be hidebound or dogmatic but can be playful in the highest sense: "A religious reading of literary texts nowadays thus would be one in which a reader understands herself as part of a community engaged in simultaneously recognizing, criticizing and reshaping the myths and rituals it lives by" (38). It takes a certain degree of *playfulness*, he notes, to reconsider the terms of one's world and to refashion one's "life narrative" accordingly, which is what religious reading, according to Detweiler, demands.

However, there is also a serious dimension to all of this, which involves acknowledging the traditions through which our religious consciousness has developed, both individually and culturally. In the following chapters we will come back to the poems of Elizabeth Bishop not as illustrations of her life but for the purpose of thinking, in religious terms, about such concepts as sin, desire, truth, charity, and self-surrender. Literature addresses these not in their abstract but in their concrete relations. And this is why it is so valuable. As William F. Lynch has written in *Christ and Apollo: The Dimensions of the Literary Imagination*: "There are no shortcuts to beauty or to insight. We must go *through* the finite, the limited, the definite, omitting none of it lest we omit some of the potencies of being-in-the-flesh" (23). Poems remind us of "the potencies of being-in-the-flesh." Like Bishop's "Imaginary Iceberg," the poem—"fleshed, fair, erected indivisible"—offers us a symbolic language with which to reconsider the conditions of our humanity. And as Lynch suggests: "Our hope must be to discover such symbols as can make the imagination *rise* indeed, and yet keep all the tang and density of that actuality into which the imagination *descends*" (33).

2

The Fall

Ashes, Ashes . . .

When I was growing up in the 1950s in Evanston, Illinois, I attended St. Luke's Episcopal Church, where each week we repeated a prayer that I still mostly know by heart and still find myself repeating in the watches of the night when I cannot sleep.

Almighty God, Father of our Lord Jesus Christ, maker of all things, judge of all men: We acknowledge and bewail our manifold sins and wickedness, which we from time to time most grievously have committed, by thought, word, and deed, against thy divine Majesty, provoking most justly thy wrath and indignation against us. We do earnestly repent, and are heartily sorry for these our misdoings; The remembrance of them is grievous unto us, the burden of them is intolerable. Have mercy upon us, have mercy upon us, most merciful Father; for thy Son our Lord Jesus Christ's sake, forgive us all that is past; and grant that we may ever hereafter serve and please thee in newness of life, to the honor and glory of thy Name; through Jesus Christ our Lord. Amen.

In many ways, of course, this antique prayer no longer speaks to us today. The language is too archaic, too patriarchal, and the vengeful side of God—wrath and indignation—is too much in the foreground. But like Elizabeth Bishop, who found herself reciting old hymns even though she wasn't quite prepared to vouch for their content, I find myself drawn back to these old prayers of my youth that, without my conscious intention, rooted themselves so firmly in my mind. The language, though no longer colloquial, is still very powerful to me. Furthermore, there is something very helpful about recognizing that we are fallen, and it is something, I am afraid, that has disappeared from many pockets of our contemporary culture. Instead of being taken seriously, as an important signal, guilt has been made into a misfortune, something to be overcome. In my view, this has led to even worse problems. It has resulted in making us attempt to deny the darker impulses of our nature, thus cutting ourselves off from what the "still, small voice" keeps telling us is our full humanity. I still remember sitting in a room filled with 300 people in the 1970s where someone said that nothing is truly evil if it is properly understood. At the time I thought there was something to be said for this position, but subsequent life experience has convinced me that this is not only nonsense, it is dangerous nonsense. Why not recognize that there are some deeds we should all condemn, knowing that under certain circumstances we might be capable of them ourselves?

Like poetry, spiritual practices can be a bulwark against the worst excesses of our time and place; by taking seriously the doctrine of the Fall, the Judeo-Christian tradition can help us to see the evil not only "out there" but "in here," in our own hearts. To come to God one must give up the illusions fostered by pride and self-justifications, a renunciation that is in itself liberating. I too have arrived at the point of saying: In truth I am a sinner, but even St. Teresa of Avila writes: "I never heard anything bad said of me which I did not *clearly* realize fell short of the truth. If I had not *sometimes—often, indeed*—offended God in the ways they referred to, I had done so in many others" (112–13). If St. Teresa can say this, what about the rest of us?

The prayers of confession are one way to cleanse ourselves and refresh our spirits so often beaten down with the misery of being who we are, imperfect and fallen. Another way is to read poetry; for example, Rainer Maria Rilke who writes:

> We all fall. This hand here falls.
> And look at others: it's in everyone.
>
> And yet there's one who holds this falling
> Infinitely gently in his hands. (Detweiler trans., 67)

In the English-speaking West we are indebted to John Milton, who in the seventeenth century gave us an enduring vision of the Fall in the poetry of *Paradise Lost*. The story of Adam and Eve that Milton constructs dramatizes the failure of free will to align itself with God's will. As soon as there is the possibility of choice, there is the possibility of error, so Eve seeks independence and power (succumbing to the serpent's wiles), and Adam fails to live up to the responsibilities of his Reason (succumbing to Eve's). Perhaps God himself is at fault in creating a situation in the first place where inequities (between angels, between Adam and Eve) breed envy, and envious feelings, already existing in the universe before the Fall, serve to unbalance the world. Perhaps the very knowledge forbidden by God is a necessary prerequisite to choosing rightly.

Whatever we think of the "sin" of eating the fruit of the tree of knowledge of good and evil, Milton is at his best in portraying the consequences of sin, which are (as they often are today) isolation, wrangling, feelings of hollowness, distortion of perspective, and self-loathing. In the aftermath of eating the apple, Adam and Eve become dissipated (literally "dis-unified"). Their frantic coupling demonstrates their realization of this. They begin to accuse one another, lose their grip on reality, and even consider suicide. Adam moans in despair:

> O Conscience, into what Abyss of fears
> And horrors hast thou driv'n me; out of which
> I find no way, from deep to deeper plunged. (Book X, ll. 842–44)

But conscience need not ally itself only with despair. It can also provide the driving force behind repentance, as it eventually does here. In their repentant state, Adam and Eve actually seem more united, more mature, more loving even of God than they did before the Fall, a point that is not lost on Christ who intercedes for them, saying:

> See Father, what first fruits on Earth are sprung
> From thy implanted Grace in Man, these sighs
> And Prayers, which in this Golden Censer, mixt
> With Incense, I thy Priest before thee bring,
> Fruits of more pleasing savor from thy seed
> Sown with contrition in his heart, than those
> Which his own hand manuring all the Trees
> Of Paradise could have produc't, ere fall'n
> From innocence. (Book XI, ll. 22–30)

The idea that, in some sense, our capacity for sin functions for our good is what is sometimes called "The Doctrine of the Fortunate Fall."

THE FORTUNATE FALL

Why should we need to be bad in order to be good? Why must we fall in order to rise? Some of us who have taken a spectacular tumble can see the logic of this trajectory quite clearly. But falling from grace is not always so precipitate. Jane Hamilton's narrator in the contemporary novel *A Map of the World* gives us a different perspective on the matter by beginning her narrative with these remarks:

> I used to think if you fell from grace it was more likely than not the result of one stupendous error, or else an unfortunate accident. I hadn't learned that it can happen so gradually you don't lose your stomach or hurt yourself in the landing. You don't necessarily sense the motion. I've found it takes at least two and generally three things to alter the course of a life. You slip around the truth once, and then again, and one more time, and there you are, feeling, for a moment, that it was sudden, your arrival at the bottom of the heap. (3)

But what about those who never do arrive at the bottom of the heap? What about those wonderful people we all know who seem to bring joy to everyone around them?

Nathaniel Hawthorne is among those classic American writers (like William Faulkner) who pondered questions about the Fall. Hawthorne cautions us against feeling that we know the secrets of the human heart. Even the most saintly, such as the Reverend Dimmesdale in *The Scarlet Letter*, may be concealing their tampering with the forbidden fruit. But Hawthorne also seems to be a proponent of the Doctrine of the Fortunate Fall. In "My Kinsman, Major Molyneux," Robin cannot become a man until he learns his own capacity for evil. And the Lord and Lady of the May in "The Maypole of Merry Mount" must give up their world of pleasure in order to follow a more difficult, postlapsarian path. Like Adam and Eve at the end of *Paradise Lost*, whose "World was all before them, where to choose / Their place of rest, and Providence their guide: / They hand in hand with wand'ring steps and slow, / Through *Eden* took their solitary way" (Book XII, ll. 646–49), the Lord and Lady of the May are expelled from Merry Mount, provoking these comments from Hawthorne's narrator:

> As the moral gloom of the world overpowers all systematic gaiety, even so was their home of wild mirth made desolate amid the sad forest. They returned to it no more. But, as their flowery garland was wreathed of the brightest roses that had grown there, so, in the tie that united them, were intertwined all the purest and best of their early joys. They went heavenward, supporting each other along the difficult path which it was their lot to tread, and never wasted one regretful thought on the vanities of Merry Mount. (183–84)

Until we feel the consequences of our transgressions, we have little motivation for learning these sad lessons. Why should we?

Poetry, however, because of its discursive power, may draw us where other forms of theology fail to. As a reader of poetry, I have found no statement about the Fall (and its sometimes fortunate consequences) that is as wonderful, as genuinely moving, as George Herbert's "Sion."

> Lord, with what glory wast thou served of old,
> When Solomon's temple stood and flourished?
>   Where most things were of purest gold;
>   The wood was all embellished
> With flowers and carvings, mystical and rare:
> All showed the builder's, craved the seer's care.
>
> Yet all this glory, all this pomp and state
> Did not affect thee much, was not thy aim;
>   Something there was, that sowed debate:
>   Wherefore thou quitt'st thy ancient claim:
> And now thy Architecture meets with sin;
> For all thy frame and fabric is within.
>
> There thou art struggling with a peevish heart,
> Which sometimes crosseth thee, thou sometimes it:
>   The fight is hard on either part.
>   Great God doth fight, he doth submit.
> All Solomon's sea of brass and world of stone
> Is not so dear to thee as one good groan.
>
> And truly brass and stones are heavy things,
> Tombs for the dead, not temples fit for thee:
>   But groans are quick, and full of wings,
>   And all their motions upward be;
> And ever as they mount, like larks they sing;
> The note is sad, yet music for a king. (98)

Here the Fall turns out to be fortunate not only for humankind but also for God who would rather have "one good groan" than all the elaborate constructions of Solomon's Disney wealth. Herbert makes our suffering seem part of a process of grace that is beneficial both to us and to God. It carries us "home," and in this poem, it carries us home with music (poetry) fit for a king.

Elizabeth Bishop loved the poetry of George Herbert, and partly she loved it because of what Jeredith Merrin calls its "enabling humility." Herbert does not preach from a position of superiority, and he is both lyrical and witty. Bishop wrote at least one poem that was consciously inspired by Herbert ("The Weed") but his influence is more pervasive than this. It also appears in Bishop's "The Fish," for example, as something Randall Jarrell described as a grave, calm, and tender form of morality, the idea that "the wickedness and confusion of the age can explain and extenuate other people's wickedness and confusion, but not, for you, your own" (Schwartz and Estess, 180). And so, in the fish poem, though one might be proud of catching the big fish, in the end, when this speaker examines what it has suffered and survived, the hooks in its jaw, the wounds on its back, she must "let the fish go."

THE PRODIGAL

Bishop had more sympathy with untidy suffering than with gloating gospels. In an amusing letter to Robert Lowell written from Wiscasset, Maine, she comments: "I've just returned from a church service at Head Tide. I guess you probably know all about it & its church, etc.— But I did leave before the sermon. I guess maybe what I don't like about this place is that its local atmosphere is so thick as to be distracting, like a fog—and of course after the rather high meat of Key West, the society is like breast of chicken" (*One Art*, 162). Key West was full of sinners, and that was one of the reasons that Elizabeth Bishop felt so comfortable there. People didn't seem to take much notice, for example, if one got drunk or in some other way stepped out of line, by failing to pay bills, say, or to meet appointments.

Yet Bishop herself was hounded by a sense of shame. Often it was caused by her alcoholism, which drove her to do things that in more sober moments she regretted. The following letter, written from Yaddo (the writer's colony in Saratoga Springs, New York), offers a heartrending example of the self-loathing that afflicts the drunkard. It was written to her doctor, Anny Baumann, to whom she was not always honest about her drinking but more honest than she was to most.

I'm going to writeyou [*sic*] a letter that I'll probably not send but maybe I'll re-read it every day as a reminder to myself. I've been having a sort of brainstorm ever since I got here, just can't stop writing, can't sleep, and although at the time I wrote before I had managed not to drink for a stretch I've certainly made up for it since & made a damn fool of myself & got into a peck of troubles.—& made a very good [friend] of mine here very unhappy.

Well, last night as the trees came crashing down all around me [in a hurricane] andI [*sic*] felt like death it seemed a sort of natural phenomena [*sic*] equal to the brainstorms and I suddenly made up my mind. I will *not* Drink. I've been stalling along now for years & it's

[absolutely] absurd. Dr. Foster said, "Well, go ahead then—ruin
your life"—and I almost have, I also know I'll go insane if I keep it up.
I *cannot* drink and I know it . . . .
    I shake so I can't sign my name. (Quoted in Millier, 228)

The most powerful poem Bishop ever wrote about her drinking
problems is "The Prodigal," mostly composed at Yaddo. "The
Prodigal" is an attempt, she said, to use the techniques suggested by
St. Ignatius in his *Spiritual Exercises* to work out the actual physical
experiences that might belong to this Biblical story. In *New King
James Bible*, Christ recounts in parable form the story of the Prodigal
Son (Luke 15:11–32), a young man who wastes his inheritance in
riotous living ("in a far country") and is forced out of necessity to
work for a farmer who keeps swine. His living conditions are so poor
that he resolves to go home and throw himself on the mercy of his
father, not expecting to be forgiven but merely to be treated as a hired
servant. However, his father has compassion for him, kills "the fatted
calf," gives him a ring, and rejoices in his return, because "one sinner
that repenteth" is a cause for "joy in the presence of the angels of
God." So this too is an example of the Fortunate Fall. The Prodigal
Son is a greater cause for celebration than his brother who stayed at
home and never transgressed.

Bishop was fascinated with this story, and, in her attempt to imagine a detailed account of the Prodigal's experiences prior to returning
home, she offers us one of the most moving portrayals of the inner life
of dissipation. The poetry intensifies our experience of the meaning of
the parable so that the Prodigal Son is no longer an abstract figure but
becomes instead a person like us. William Lynch analyzes the "applica-
tion of the senses" in the *Spiritual Exercises* (from which Bishop in a
letter to Robert Lowell said she built her poem). According to
Ignatius, we must fully imagine the sights, sounds, feelings, smells, and
tastes that made up the life of Jesus, and Lynch comments that the
detailed "composition of place" that Ignatius recommends is at one
and the same time thoroughly concrete and thoroughly poetic. Poetry
too, he says, requires the reader to live dramatically in the space of the
poem's physical details, so it provides the same type of intense realization
of experience that the spiritual exercises are meant to evoke.

Bishop found Ignatius's instructions compelling, and here, in her
evocation of the fall of the Prodigal, we can see why, as she makes us
feel what Milton's Satan meant when he said, "Myself am Hell."

The brown enormous odor he lived by
was too close, with its breathing and thick hair,

for him to judge. The floor was rotten; the sty
was plastered halfway up with glass-smooth dung.
Light-lashed, self-righteous, above moving snouts,
the pigs' eyes followed him, a cheerful stare—
even to the sow that always ate her young—
till, sickening, he leaned to scratch her head.
But sometimes mornings after drinking bouts
(he hid the pints behind a two-by-four),
the sunrise glazed the barnyard mud with red;
the burning puddles seemed to reassure.
And then he thought he almost might endure
his exile yet another year or more.

But evenings the first star came to warn.
The farmer whom he worked for came at dark
to shut the cows and horses in the barn
beneath their overhanging clouds of hay,
with pitchforks, faint forked lightnings, catching light,
safe and companionable as in the Ark.
The pigs stuck out their little feet and snored.
The lantern—like the sun, going away—
laid on the mud a pacing aureole.
Carrying a bucket along a slimy board,
he felt the bats' uncertain staggering flight,
his shuddering insights, beyond his control,
touching him. But it took him a long time
finally to make his mind up to go home. (*CP*, 71)

Bishop said that many of her poems took the form of parables, and
this poem, like "Roosters," which we will examine in due course, is
clearly one of these. Parables are teaching stories but they require
reflection in order to get at the teaching, as centuries of sermons on
Christ's parables illustrate. What is the teaching of this poem, one
might ask? Is it really about sin or something else?

Though many pastors still proclaim that alcoholism is indeed a sin,
that view is less prominent today than it once was. We tend to believe
that alcoholics are afflicted, prone to their "disease" because of
a genetic predisposition or because of their childhood experiences. We
pity them, as indeed we should, because they seem to be without
the resources to renounce their destructive habits. Bishop herself felt
that her family genealogy (father, grandfather, uncles) contributed to
her alcoholism, and further that her relationship with her mother
during her early years cemented the link to that inheritance.

It is not my purpose here to take up the contested issue of whether
excessive drinking is itself a sin or whether it is a disease to which one

is subject by virtue of one's nature or upbringing. It seems to me quite possible to believe that both are true. One reading of *Paradise Lost* asserts that Eve was not prepared to avoid the Fall as she had not been created with the requisite tools to resist her tempter; furthermore, she could not foresee the consequences of her actions since there was no precedent to the Fall in Eden. Nevertheless, she sinned. We all have our stories about the chain of events that led us to our transgressions; most of us feel helpless in the face of our greatest temptations and wonder in the aftermath if we could have done otherwise.

The point of "The Prodigal" is not blame. To a greater or lesser extent the Fall is something we all experience, whether we are drunkards or not. Excessive drinking is not necessarily "evil"—certainly not in the conventional sense—but it draws people into its web, contributing to betrayals, violence, and self-destructive behavior. For all her self-justifications, Bishop was well aware of this, and that is why she felt so ashamed. In her letter to Anny Baumann, she speaks of making a good friend "very unhappy," and for Bishop this was certainly something to regret.

Is there a positive side to this dark scenario? The title of the poem suggests that there might be, since the word "prodigal" is itself a gesture toward the notion of the Fortunate Fall, meaning both (1) wasteful, reckless, and (2) abundant, giving or yielding profusely. By removing the word "Son," which was there in earlier drafts, the reader's attention is focused on the word "prodigal" itself with its double emphasis, fortune and fall.

The heart of the poem is not about whether we should blame the toper for his unseemly behavior. What we experience when we read the poem is the terrible inner life of dissipation, and it is strikingly similar to Milton's portrayal of Adam and Eve after the Fall: full of isolation, feelings of hollowness, distortion of perspective, and self-loathing. There is even a hint of wrangling when the farmer appears, showing concern for his animals but without a word for his servant who is locked out of the "safe and companionable" Ark. Is the farmer God and is the Prodigal bitter that he has been excluded from grace? It is certainly a possibility.

"The brown enormous odor he lived by" makes it impossible for the Prodigal to judge accurately. That brown enormous odor could, of course, be created by the pigs, but it could also be furnished by the booze (Bishop's favorite drink was bourbon) for it is booze that, in another sense, "he lived by," becoming in the details of the poem a kind of monster "with its breathing and thick hair."

Jonathan Edwards's famous sermon, "Sinners in the Hands of an Angry God," characterizes the unrepentant sinner as one who walks on a rotten floor that any minute might give way, dropping him directly into Hell, and here too "the floor was rotten." Simone Weil captures this idea in a more modern form by writing that when a man turns away from God, "he simply gives himself up to the law of gravity" (128). The Prodigal seems to be in perpetual free fall where even his physical circumstances—red mud, burning puddles, glinting pitchforks—are distorted and hellish. Like Satan in *Paradise Lost*, he sometimes finds this world compatible ("the burning puddles seemed to reassure") but that word "seemed" is premonitory. He is alone, he is deluded, he is an exile; he is at risk.

Even the pigs seem to despise him, watching him cheerfully with "light-lashed, self-righteous eyes," even down to the sow "that always ate her young." The fact that others are also sinful brings no satisfaction, though, especially when one is despised by the self-righteous, a term that in Bishop's mind often characterized Christians ("mostly on their way to being fascists"). Part of the Prodigal seems to like the pigs, seems to feel akin, so that when he vomits over the railing ("sickening," Bishop calls it, in a tumbling verb), he also reaches down to scratch the sow's head. Cannibals all, pigs united.

The poem rises to a crescendo in the last seven lines, beginning with the lantern at sunset that lays "on the mud a pacing aureole." What could make us feel more profoundly the horror of the Prodigal's plight than the fact that "Carrying a bucket along a slimy board" (slimy with vomit? slimy with slops?), "he felt the bats' uncertain staggering flight, / his shuddering insights, beyond his control, touching him"? His thoughts are like bats, fearful dive-bombers that afflict him; and they remind us of Bishop's "brainstorms" at Yaddo, which she characterized as beyond her control.

If we are going to let the poem work on us, we have to be willing to let ourselves participate in the misery of the Prodigal's life. A lot, of course, depends upon how we read the last lines: "But it took him a long time / finally to make his mind up to go home." Skeptical readers will emphasize that there is no sign of grace in the poem, no change of heart helped by the Lord's intervention. Furthermore, we don't know what it means when finally the Prodigal makes up his mind to go home. As a modern poem disengaged from the biblical text, it may suggest that he is merely going back to his hovel to begin his life of alcoholic dissipation anew the very next day. This is not the Prodigal Son, after all, but merely the Prodigal, a man cut off from all signs of family history or providential return.

However, it is also possible, without doing violence to the poem itself, to read the ending as hopeful. We might take the "But" as suggesting a radical disjunction from the misery of repetition, affirmed by the continuous present of "sometimes mornings," "evenings," words to capture a life that goes on day after day in a pigsty. When the Prodigal *Son* goes home, we know what happens. The fact that here, after a long litany of suffering, there is an assertion of will, when the prodigal at last makes up his mind to go home, might signal the kind of change in behavior that Bishop herself wanted to make when she wrote to Anny Baumann, "I *will* not Drink." That she wasn't able to stick to it does not contradict the fact that many alcoholics (some with the help of a Higher Power) do go on the wagon and transform their lives. Change *is* possible when there is the will to change, but where is this effective will to come from if not from God? All we know is that at the end of the poem, the Prodigal makes "his mind up to go home."

There was a lot, for Bishop, in that word "home." And for many of us as well. How rare it is to find a home that completely fulfills our longings for unconditional love; for total understanding and respect; for security without boredom. In the *Oxford English Dictionary*, which Bishop was fond of consulting, the very meanings of the word "home" are a reprimand, reminding us of how often the reality of home mocks the language of our fantasies of it as "a place, region or state to which one properly belongs, in which one's affections center, where one finds refuge, rest, or satisfaction." Home should be "an institution providing refuge or rest for the destitute, the afflicted, the infirm, etc., or for those who either have no home of their own, or are obliged by their vocation to live at a distance from the home of their family." To go home means to go "to the very heart or root of a matter; into close and effective contact; so as to touch, reach, or affect intimately; closely, effectively, thoroughly, out and out." But too many of us are exiles. Even the nature of our language, the inevitable distance between signifier and signified, is a confession of our homelessness.

Elizabeth Bishop, of course, knew the feeling of homelessness better than many, having lost both her parents by the age of five, then having been placed and displaced among relatives, making her, even in her adult life, mostly a wanderer. Robert Lowell remembers her saying to him in 1948: "When you write my epitaph, you must say I was the loneliest person who ever lived" (Millier, 203). For a poet who wrote so often about domesticity, Bishop wrote few poems that convey a sense of home, one of them being "The Shampoo," written during the early years with Lota de Macedo Soares, the only person who gave her, for a few years at least, the sense of truly having a home.

But even Lota, dear Lota, was at times unkind, excoriating Bishop about her drinking, taunting her about her small literary output, and in the end punishing her (if Bishop was right) by taking an overdose of pills right in her (borrowed) apartment, so that Bishop, who witnessed her lover tumble down in the kitchen, was in a real sense left "to take the fall." She was blamed by many who believed that Lota's suicide was Elizabeth's fault. Even those we love most sometimes fail us. In Bishop's "Varick Street" the refrain repeats: "*And I shall sell you sell you / sell you of course, my dear, and you'll sell me*" (*CP*, 75–76).

Where can we turn when we feel that deep sense of homelessness? The God who offers us shelter, the God who loves and forgives, who "gave His only begotten Son that we might not perish but have everlasting life," is, for persons of the Christian faith, the one who fulfills in every respect this desire for Home. In such a God, the Fall need not be a permanent affliction. But first we need to acknowledge "where we are at." And where we are at, it seems, is in the soup, in what Allen Ginsberg calls "the total animal soup of time" ("Howl," 16). Though in the United States, we are currently experiencing a profound sense of ourselves as belonging to a particular country and history, even nations may be fallen; ours, with its history of slavery and Indian massacres, support for dictators, political assassinations, and the bombing of Hiroshima, has certainly at times failed to live up to its vaunted ideals. Instead of being self-righteous about what it means to be "American," perhaps it would be more proper if, like Marianne Moore, we too were "in distrust of merits."

ROOSTERS

In "Roosters," Elizabeth Bishop wrote about where the world was at and gave no quarter. Though written during the Second World War, there isn't a glimmer of patriotic fervor to be found in it, despite the fact that Bishop did war work (briefly) and certainly was no friend to either the Fascists or, for that matter, the Communists, two groups she tended to conflate. The poem is not history, however, but parable, a parable we would do well to heed at this particularly vexed political moment.

In the first half of this five-page poem (*CP*, 35–39), we have the parable of the combative roosters whose cries express the essence of militarism from Bishop's point of view:

> Cries galore
> come from the water-closet door,
> from the dropping-plastered henhouse floor,

where in the blue blur
their rustling wives admire,
the roosters brace their cruel feet and glare

with stupid eyes
while from their beaks there rise
the uncontrolled, traditional cries.

Deep from protruding chests
in green-gold medals dressed,
planned to command and terrorize the rest,

the many wives
who lead hens' lives
of being courted and despised;

deep from raw throats
a senseless order floats
all over town. (*CP*, 35)

It's a wonderful form, this three-line stanza, with its repeating end rhymes mimicking the rooster cries erupting from various parts of the early dawn's "blue blur"; sometimes the rhyme-cries are echoes (full rhymes), sometimes not. At first it is comparatively easy to see that these cocks are the bad guys: coldhearted womanizers, terrorizing the rest of the world with their angry insistence on their own way, acting just like "men": "Each one an active / displacement in perspective: / Each screaming, 'This is where I live!' / Each screaming / 'Get up! Stop dreaming!' " so that when the punning line occurs—"Roosters, what are you projecting?"—we are quite prepared to read the roosters as an animal substitution for these male militarists, projecting cries, projecting bombs ("projectiles"); projecting, in the Freudian sense, their own fears of inadequacy upon demonized "others" who can then be destroyed.

> The crown of red
> set on your little head
> is charged with all your fighting blood.

That coxcomb is certainly very phallic:

> Yes, that excrescence
> makes a most virile presence,
> plus all that vulgar beauty of iridescence.

We see the Fall played out literally, as a cockfight meant to suggest a "dogfight."

> Now in mid-air
> by twos they fight each other.
> Down comes a first flame-feather,

and one is flying,
with raging heroism defying
even the sensation of dying.

And one has fallen,
but still above the town
his torn-out, bloodied feathers drift down.

In fact, this "fall" is what provides the hinge between the two parts of the poem that seem to be so different. For, once having spelled out the parable of the roosters, the poem rather suddenly moves into a different register.

St. Peter's sin
was worse than that of Magdalen
whose sin was of the flesh alone;

of spirit, Peter's,
falling, beneath the flares,
among the "servants and officers."

After the parable of the roosters, we are suddenly in the Bible. And now, rather than emblems of militarism, the cocks become sacred icons, once again suggestive of the Doctrine of the Fortunate Fall. We hear about a painting (Millier identifies it as one by Caravaggio) where Peter and Christ stand side by side, "both as if dazed," while in between a sculpted cock reminds us of Peter's betrayal of Christ signaled by the cock's crowing. Peter's tears, bespeaking repentance, inspire a very different response than the "very combative" roosters that earlier provoked the speaker to ask: "what right have you to give / commands and tell us how to live, / cry 'Here!' and 'Here!' / and wake us here where are / unwanted love, conceit, and war?"

In the second part of the poem, there is something that wasn't there before, which Bishop calls "inescapable hope, the pivot." Indeed our speaker urges us as readers to return to the Fall and see it in a different light: "Poor Peter, heart-sick, / still cannot guess / those cock-a-doodles yet might bless, / his dreadful rooster come to mean forgiveness."

A second artistic image of the rooster—"a bronze cock on a porphyry / pillar"—stands outside the Church of St. John Lateran in Rome:

So the people and the Pope might see
that even the Prince
of the Apostles long since
had been forgiven, and to convince

all the assembly
that "Deny deny deny"
is not all the roosters cry.

Wake up, wake up, the roosters say, even in their unselfconscious
moments of simple virile display. As with Rilke's "Archaic Bust of
Apollo," the significance we instinctively feel in the artist's rendering
of the rooster is not the anger of denial but our own need to heed the
message "You must change your life." Sometimes Art, by means of its
confounding beauty, can serve the function of religion even without
the mythology. Sometimes nature or love or even our enemies can
wake us. So we must go back to the first half of the poem, where the
speaker herself is in denial, fuming: "What right have you to give commands and tell us how to live." If we are careful readers, we should
pause, however, when we hear that the roosters "wake us here where
are / unwanted love, conceit, and war."

Unwanted love, I am afraid, is a euphemism for rape and not a very
happy one, but perhaps this is intentional, because it demonstrates the
desire (even for the speaker) not to confront ugly realities. But we had
better wake up if "here where [we] are" rape, pride, and murderous
competition are in the ascendancy.

NEW, TENDER, AND QUICK

Before we belabor this poem too much, however, it is worth remembering that Elizabeth Bishop did not like heaviness. In a long letter to
Anne Stevenson (January 8, 1964), she said exactly that ("I do not
like *heaviness*"), adding: "I think one can be cheerful and profound."
Her view, she admitted, was pessimistic. "I think we are still barbarians, barbarians who commit a hundred indecencies and cruelties
every day of our lives, as just possibly future ages may be able to see.
But I think we should be gay in spite of it, sometimes even giddy—to
make life endurable and to keep ourselves 'new, tender, quick' "
(unpublished letter, WU Archive). To underscore the spiritual dimension of this process, she provides a reference in her final words here to
"Love Unknown" by George Herbert.

"Roosters" is not a heavy poem. It's not preachy, despite its attention
to serious issues, and there is a lot of wit in it, even in the way the
rhymes are handled. In an early section of the poem, for instance, the
warlike roosters are described as:

making sallies
from all the muddy alleys
marking out maps like Rand McNally's;

The way these three lines build up is almost funny, almost a form of burlesque. And when the speaker asks archly, "Roosters, what are you projecting?"—this is very tongue in cheek, it seems to me. But we shouldn't make the mistake of confusing Bishop's humor with derision. An exchange of letters with Jane Shore demonstrates that Bishop made an important distinction in her own mind between teasing and deriding. In her excellent essay "Elizabeth Bishop: The Art of Changing Your Mind," Shore talks about the way Bishop changes churches into arrowheads in "Cape Breton," commenting: "On a more serious level, this symbolic gesture is an oblique swipe at the organized religion that Bishop systematically derides" (182). However, in her unpublished letter to Shore (May 10, 1979), Bishop took issue with this statement: "The only remark I'd take exception to is on page 182—that I 'systematically deride' 'organized religion.' I never meant to do that—& again, on page 190, when I speak of the 'miracle' [in 'Santarém']—I'm repeating what was told me, and I suppose making fun a little of the local simplicities—but I hope I wasn't deriding . . ." (Vassar Archive).

Breaking away from heaviness, as well as from derision, the ending of "Roosters" returns the poem to its local atmosphere—a morning in Key West. Everything is so pretty in the morning light that the speaker wonders "how could the night have come to grief?" Only in the last two stanzas do the darker tones of the earlier parts of the poem intrude.

> In the morning
> a low light is floating
> in the backyard, and gilding
>
> from underneath
> the broccoli, leaf by leaf;
> how could the night have come to grief?
>
> gilding the tiny
> floating swallow's belly
> and lines of pink cloud in the sky,
>
> the day's preamble
> like wandering lines in marble.
> The cocks are now almost inaudible.
>
> The sun climbs in,
> following "to see the end,"
> faithful as enemy, or friend. (*CP*, 39)

The point here, it seems to me, is *as lightly as possible* (note the ebbing away of exact rhymes toward the end) to suggest the presence of God (here manifest as beauty) in lives that are full of pain. As the morning takes hold, the cocks become *almost* inaudible. The light is perhaps a false "gilding" of the situation (after all there *was* a certain amount of violence in the night), but it is beautiful nonetheless. Particularly unexpected is the image of the shreds of cloud "like wandering lines in marble," yet these "lines" have a curious relation to other "lines" in Bishop's work, to the "gray scratches / like the admirable scriptures made on stones by stones" in "Cape Breton," to "the lines [of etching] that move apart / like ripples above sand, dispersing storms, God's spreading fingerprint" in Bishop's poem on the Bible, "Over 2,000 Illustrations and a Complete Concordance." In the dust jacket blurb Bishop wrote for Robert Lowell's *Life Studies*, she remembers: "As a child, I used to look at my grandfather's Bible under a powerful reading-glass. The letters assembled beneath the lens were suddenly like a Lowell poem, as big as life and as alive, and rainbow-edged" (Schwartz and Estess, 285). These "wandering lines" of cloud seem as much as anything to be God's signature, written in an illegible hand, but big as life and possibly rainbow-edged, none theless. To a mind willing to see spiritual significance in the material world (what Christians of an earlier era called "correspondences"), these dispersing clouds "like wandering lines in marble" recall us to Marianne Moore's conclusion: "Beauty is everlasting / and dust is for a time."

At the end of "Roosters," the sun climbs in "to see the end." The allusion is to Matthew 26:58 where, after Jesus has been arrested, Peter follows "to see the end." Though he has already failed to live up to his promise to Jesus to stay awake in the Garden of Gethsemane, Peter will also, after the trial, refuse three times to acknowledge his relationship to Christ, and then the cock crows. "And Peter remembered the word of Jesus who had said to him, 'Before the rooster crows, you will deny Me three times.' So he went out and wept" (Matt. 26:75). But the moment at which he follows the officers to the courtyard of Caiaphas "to see the end," occurs *between* these two sequences, the first in the garden and the second in the street. In other words, he has fallen once and he will fall again, but in this act of witnessing—where he watches "to see the end"—he nevertheless demonstrates his faithfulness. "Deny deny deny" is not all the roosters cry. They usher in Peter's sense of fallen-ness, which is, in a sense, his salvation.

When, at the end of Bishop's poem, the sun climbs in " 'to see the end,' / faithful as enemy, or friend," the sun is like the roosters, serving a double purpose, reminding us that that we are still barbarians (as Bishop put it) but also offering what she calls "inescapable hope, the pivot." As Peter was both friend and enemy to Jesus in the Gospel of Matthew, the light of truth (the sun) reveals us in all our freckled nature. What should we say, except what T. S. Eliot says in "Ash Wednesday": "For what is done, not to be done again / May the judgment not be too heavy upon us" (86).

3

LOVE AND LONGING

PUTTING LOVE INTO ACTION

In the Fall we are broken, but with Love we find the promise of healing. This is the message of the gospels, but many of us have experienced this quite outside of any religious context; we simply come into the presence of love bareheaded with all our wounds apparent. When I fell in love with my husband, I had at the time no religious affiliation, and yet what I profoundly felt was that we were one soul that God had cut apart, a little off center perhaps, creating a bigger and a smaller half. Now, it seemed, we would reunite the parts and all my scars would disappear.

It is not, I think, an uncommon experience to be drawn by the experience of love into the realm of God. I like the way Jeanette Winterson captures this equivocal motion of the heart in her novel *The Passion*. Her protagonist, aptly named "Villanelle," is an artist, a Venetian casino dealer with webbed feet, a pickpocket whose gender is a performance in defiance of her sex and whose down-to-earth perspective prior to falling in love gives her a foolish sense of invulnerability: "I am pragmatic about love and have taken my pleasure with both men and women, but I have never needed a guard for my heart. My heart is a reliable organ" (33). Love, that is "passion," finds her out, however, destroying her naïve complacency. "How is it," she asks, "that one day life is orderly and you are content, a little cynical perhaps but on the whole just so, and then without warning you find the solid floor is a trapdoor and you are now in another place whose geography is uncertain and whose customs are strange?" (49).

Villanelle is not a believer, at least not in a churchgoing sense, but in the aftermath of falling in love she is drawn to the churches of Venice, making the connection explicit between different kinds of love and longing.

I never go to confession; God doesn't want us to confess, he wants us to challenge him, but for a while I went into our churches because they were built from the heart. Improbable hearts that I had never understood before. Hearts so full of longing that these old stones still cry out with the ecstasy. These are warm churches, built in the sun.

I sat at the back, listening to the music or mumbling through the service. I'm never tempted by God but I like his trappings. Not tempted but I begin to understand why others are. With this feeling inside, with this wild love that threatens, what safe places might there be? Where do you store gunpowder? How do you sleep at night again? If I were a little different I might turn passion into something holy and then I would sleep again. And then my ecstasy would be my ecstasy but I would not be afraid. (39–40)

This character is a Romantic, of course, and thus unlike what we mostly understand about Elizabeth Bishop. And yet Villanelle's language of travel is highly reminiscent of Bishop's psychological geography. Winterson's character is not literally a traveler. She says: "Travellers at least have a choice. Those who set sail know that things will not be the same as at home. Explorers are prepared. But for us, who travel along the blood vessels, who come to the cities of the interior by chance, there is no preparation. We who were fluent find life is a foreign language. Somewhere between the swamp and the mountains. Somewhere between fear and sex. Somewhere between God and the Devil, passion is and the way there is sudden and the way back is worse" (49–50).

Bishop, too, was a passionate person, a "traveler" interested in the ambiguous motions of the heart. "We leave Santos [the harbor] at once"; she writes in *Questions of Travel*, "we are driving to the interior" (*CP*, 90). There is no safe harbor in Bishop any more than there is in Winterson. Both live on their nerves, but it is sometimes possible to read Bishop's poems of longing not only as records of failed love affairs but also as religious poems. Villanelle speaks of passion as making it impossible to sleep; in Bishop's "Insomnia" we find her longing for a world of "otherness" in which the realm of everyday reality might be inverted and Love become a presence rather than an absence.

The moon presides over this world of illusion, but the moon might be understood here as an imagined version of lesbian transcendence. In any case, she's a figure to be reckoned with who illuminates a world of difference.

By the Universe deserted,
she'd tell it to go to hell,
and she'd find a body of water,

or a mirror, on which to dwell.

So wrap up care in a cobweb
and drop it down the well

into that world inverted
where left is always right,
where the shadows are really the body,
where we stay awake all night,
where the heavens are shallow as the sea
is now deep, and you love me. (*CP*, 70)

This poem has fascinated many a Bishop reader, though no one, I suspect, has wanted to think of it as a poem about longing for God. Its lesbian overtones are more readily accessible: for example, in the image of the well (*The Well of Loneliness* being one of the most famous lesbian novels of this time) and the use of the verb "inverted," which evokes the term "invert," a psychoanalytic, "sexologist" reference to the homosexual still in use in the mid-twentieth century.

Is it possible, then, to argue that one might *also* find in this playful musing about lost love a spiritual hunger? There is ample evidence that Bishop did feel "deserted" by God, which is why Jeredith Merrin claims that "her personal losses are persistently bound up with a sense of vanished orthodox Christian belief" (9). "Paris, 7 A.M." speaks of the empty sky as emblematic of the death of God: "This sky is no carrier-warrior-pigeon / escaping endless intersecting circles. / It is a dead one, or the sky from which a dead one fell" (*CP*, 26). We are denied transcendence, Bishop says here, and left instead with "endless intersecting circles," trivial repetitive loves.

In "Insomnia" the moon is similarly deserted by the Universe (note the capitalization), but through the imagination this speaker finds a substitute that sounds suspiciously like another version of the same. The place where "the shadows are really the body" is a place deeply inflected by religious rhetoric of shadow and substance. One of Coleman Barks's translations of Rumi makes an apt companion piece to this poem where he says:

When I am with you, we stay awake all night.
When you're not here, I can't go to sleep.

Praise God for these two insomnias!
And the difference between them. (*The Essential Rumi*, 106)

In Rumi's work, love is always both carnal and spiritual. But what about those perplexing last two lines in Bishop's poem: "where the heavens are shallow as the sea / is now deep, and you love me"?

As I read them, I hear the ghostly presence of the twenty-third psalm because of the nature of the mixed meter. In the psalm you find an uneven pattern of stresses at the beginning, ending with three strongly stressed words: "The *Lord* is my *shep*herd. *I shall not want.*" Similarly, in Bishop you have this uneven pattern concluding with three strongly stressed words: "where the *heav*ens are *shall*ow *as* the *sea* is now *deep* . . . and *you love me.*" It's not absolutely parallel, but in a poet's ear there might be an echo, especially with *shall* and *shallow.*

But what about the meaning of Bishop's lines? I keep remembering her delight in Rimbaud's image of eternity as "the sea gone off with the sun." If the world of loss is imaginatively compensated here, in a place "where the heavens are shallow as the sea is now deep," perhaps what we have is an imagined world of convergence, heaven come down to earth, with *this* world (rather than eternity) assuming a depth and meaningfulness that might be summed up as love.

What makes Bishop's poetry so attractive to readers for whom religious certainties have been lost is precisely this recognition that such depth and meaningfulness must be the result of our own effort, here the effort of the imagination but one might also speak about the effort of faith. In Bishop's world, love requires repeated activity not just feeling. In "Chemin de Fer," the old hermit screams "Love should be put into action!" But we know about this hermit. He's a part of all of us, his pond "an old tear / holding on to its injuries/ lucidly year after year." He wants the world (or God) to make it up to him. Love should be put into action, by someone (or something) else. But this leaves him looking into a mirror of endless narcissistic reflection:

> "Love should be put into action!"
> screamed the old hermit.
> Across the pond an echo
> tried and tried to confirm it. (*CP*, 8)

Is the lack of any confirmation the fault of Love, or of a certain kind of selfish longing that keeps looking elsewhere for compensation? The sentiment of self.

George Herbert has an interesting "take" on the way an exaggerated sense of self works to frustrate the operations of Love in "Love III," the poem that induced in Simone Weil the vision of Christ as a physical presence. Bishop admitted that she used Herbert as a way of inhabiting the mind of a believer even though she herself could never quite believe. She also recounted the story of Weil's mystical vision with a good deal of relish because it came out of the recitation of a poem, a poem Bishop herself was fond of rereading and could probably also recite, since her memory for poetry was prodigious.

> Love bade me welcome: yet my soul drew back,
>   Guilty of dust and sin.
> But quick-eyed Love, observing me grow slack
>   From my first entrance in,
> Drew nearer to me, sweetly questioning,
>   If I lacked anything.
>
> A guest, I answered, worthy to be here:
>   Love said, You shall be he.
> I the unkind, ungrateful? Ah my dear,
>   I cannot look on thee.
> Love took my hand, and smiling did reply,
>   Who made the eyes but I?
>
> Truth Lord, but I have marred them: let my shame
>   Go where it doth deserve.
> And know you not, says Love, who bore the blame?
>   My dear, then I will serve.
> You must sit down, says Love, and taste my meat:
>   So I did sit and eat. (178)

There is something very funny about this poem. Love is trying to give this speaker a gift, but the speaker keeps saying "Oh, I really couldn't accept. I'm really not good enough," until finally Love says, in effect, "Why do you keep talking about yourself all the time? Shut up and eat."

This little parable has a lot of resonance in the several realms of love and longing we are trying to connect here. One knows so many people who are constantly looking for a loving partner, and yet when someone comes along who actually offers love, the reaction is not infrequently one of recoil. Longing preserves the integrity of the lover whereas love threatens it. In religious life the same is true. We would rather run away from God than stand still and find ourselves both possessed and undone.

For many, longing *is* the experience of love because it seems so active and full of feeling. It is also said to be the impetus behind poetry: "Longing alone is singer to the lute," wrote Edna St. Vincent Millay Like Bishop herself, many poets are lonely people whose emotional life is full of that sense of something missing, which is captured lyrically in the Bible in the "Song of Songs." In the Hebrew text the soul is constantly searching for God, knocking on doors, asking the watchman. "By night on my bed I sought him whom my soul loveth: I sought him, but I found him not," says the biblical writer in chapter three of the "Song of Solomon." The songs provide some of the most beautiful poetry in the Bible and they are full of longing. Fulfillment breathes, it seems, but hunger sings.

Herbert's narrator in "Love III" is also initially consumed by a sense of loss and inadequacy. He is not "up to" being found; he *won't have it*, as it were. He'd rather serve than eat. But Love takes possession of him: "You must sit down, says Love, and taste my meat." The meat is the hard part, as I understand it. Partly, it's simply the heart of the matter, as in "the meat of the nut," its center and substance. But we need teeth to eat meat. It cannot be fed to infants in its natural state. To eat the meat of Love requires giving up the pleasures of longing, something Villanelle—a worshipper at passion's altar—is not required to do, since her lover is in a real sense unavailable. In Herbert's poem, too, accepting Love silences the speaker. The ending—"So I did sit and eat"—is an abrupt curtailment at which point the curtain of physical intimacy is allowed to fall. The speaker seems to have a premonition about the way Love will "cut him off" because he shrinks in its presence: "But quick-eyed Love, observing me grow slack / From my first entrance in / Drew nearer to me, sweetly questioning, / If I lacked anything." It's hard to give up the notion that life is all about us, *our* needs, *our* losses, *our* limits. But what if it isn't? "Know you not, says Love, who bore the blame?"

THE FILLING STATION

Many critics say that Elizabeth Bishop refuses the kind of religious consolation offered by George Herbert. But in her poetry there are moments of uncanny irruption, what Anne Stevenson calls "epiphanic showings forth." We find them in "The Moose," "The Weed," "Santarém," and in "Filling Station," which seems a particularly good poem to think about in terms of love and longing. Both are present there and the balance between them, or the imbalance, though not resolved, is nevertheless suggestive.

> Oh, but it is so dirty!
> —this little filling station,
> oil-soaked, oil-permeated
> to a disturbing, over-all
> black transparency.
> Be careful with that match!
>
> Father wears a dirty,
> oil-soaked monkey suit

that cuts him under the arms,
and several quick and saucy
and greasy sons assist him
(it's a family filling station),
all quite thoroughly dirty.

Do they live in the station?
It has a cement porch
behind the pumps, and on it
a set of crushed and grease-
impregnated wickerwork;
on the wicker sofa
a dirty dog, quite comfy.

Some comic books provide
the only note of color—
of certain color. They lie
upon a big dim doily
draping a taboret
(part of the set), beside
a big hirsute begonia.

Why the extraneous plant?
Why the taboret?
Why, oh why, the doily?
(Embroidered in daisy stitch
with marguerites, I think,
and heavy with gray crochet.)

Somebody embroidered the doily.
Somebody waters the plant,
or oils it, maybe. Somebody
arranges the rows of cans
so that they softly say:
ESSO—SO—SO—SO
to high-strung automobiles.
Somebody loves us all. (*CP*, 127–28)

This seems to me to be a poem about "home" as seen by an outsider, Bishop herself. As such it is full of longing, but, strangely, this longing is not filtered through pain. At the "filling station"—a wonderful metaphor for the homely revitalizing love one gets at home—even this observer, it seems, can refuel.

I must say that I find it bizarre that some readers feel panic and distress in this poem. Guy Rotella, for example, whose chapter on Bishop in *Reading and Writing Nature* I mostly admire, says some good things about "Somebody loves us all," calling it a "litany: like the repeated 'SO,' a quiet prayer" (192). But then he veers off into what seems to me to be a reading overdetermined by extraneous beliefs about Bishop herself, her early losses and her religious skepticism. Here is a chunk of that argument

> As comforting details accumulate, so does the speaker's distress about their source: "Why the extraneous plant? / Why the taboret? / Why, oh why, the doily?" The origin of this distress is partly autobiographical, since Bishop's mother was lost to her when Bishop was very young. The disturbance has an esthetic source as well. Those patterned "so's" almost spell S.O.S.; Bishop thought "an element of mortal panic and fear" underlies "all works of art." Psychological, epistemological, and theological issues are also involved: the speaker's distress reflects the loss of the nurturing mother, and the difficulties of "reading" the work of any absent designer, human or divine. Presence is known only through signs; the signs are nearly obscured and all but impossible to read; they may be accidents, or projections of the self. (192)

Well, I say, yes and no. By the time I get to the end, I don't feel any panic whatever in this poem. And when I read these questions—"Why the extraneous plant? / Why the taboret? / Why, oh why, the doily?" — it seems to me perfectly possible to imagine that the poet is dissolving in a moment of private hilarity because, from a certain point of view, these homely attempts at decorating are so incongruous. Why *would* you put a white doily in such an oily environment?

However, this question is not meant to fill us with dismay. Quite the contrary, it gives rise to a quiet form of respect for the futile optimism manifested by these efforts. Bishop loved the way people with very few means demonstrated their faith in life. Even Rotella is willing to acknowledge this, where he says: "The Esso cans speak 'softly.' They represent the sort of unassuming art that Bishop most respects, art that offers some minimal pattern to moderate soiled life without making false claims or grandiose assertions" (191).

If we compare this filling station with Wilson's garage in F. Scott Fitzgerald's *The Great Gatsby*, a book we know Bishop read, we find that both are greasy and presided over by somewhat "reduced" male figures. The father here wears a "monkey suit" that cuts him under the arms. Both are family operations where the business owners live on the property. But there the similarity ends. In *The Great Gatsby*, Myrtle's volcanic sexual energy defies the idea of family and is always threatening to explode, while here the "disturbing" element mentioned in the first stanza (the oily patina that gives rise to the warning "Be careful with that match!") is gradually overwritten by further perceptions: the monkey suit fades into its echo, a "big, hirsute begonia"; the dirty dog, after all, looks "quite comfy"; and the rows of cans offer soothing words to "high-strung automobiles." According to one critic, the phrase "so-so-so" was used to calm horses in Nova Scotia. By the time we get to "Somebody loves us all," we should be smiling, it seems to me, not panicking.

This poem is an example of what Bishop said she admired about the baroque poets: their capacity for capturing "not a thought, but the mind thinking" (*One Art*, 12). Her favorite exemplars of the baroque were George Herbert and Gerard Manley Hopkins, because in each the "truth" is postponed in favor of an unfolding process of perception that furnishes the poem with its freshness and surprise. Thomas Travisano comments: "Surprise, that access to delight, is the favorite antidote to self-pity in [Bishop's] writing" (12).

To return to the question of love and longing—how do they play out in this poem?—one would have to say that there *is* longing here, because there is something very snug and strangely nurturing about this environment, something that at first leaves the speaker out of its circle of warm associations. The men seemed blessed by an unseen presence; Rotella tentatively names it "mother as God?"

COMIC RELIEF

The mode of longing in literature, however, is usually pathos, and pathos is undercut here by the comic element, first signaled by the comic books themselves, intensified by the marguerites embroidered in "gray crochet," and then detonated by the lines: "Somebody waters the plant, / or oils it, maybe." There's nothing really disturbing about these lines. By means of surprise—which Travisano rightly notes gives us access to delight—we have passed from pathos to comedy, from longing to love.

One can certainly accept Rotella's proposition that "presence is known only through signs; the signs are nearly obscured and all but impossible to read; they may be accidents or projections of the self." This is simply a statement about the human condition, isn't it? I also agree that the final line—"Somebody loves us all"—should not be read as a pious coda telling us what we should believe. But, for me at least, there is no bitterness in it. One way of reading this line is to say that the speaker's feeling *at the particular moment recorded here*, and produced by the series of impressions she has shared with us, her process of thought, is best summarized in this way. Her mind is not fixed but moving, and here it is moving toward love.

Of course, the speaker is also soon to leave the filling station—she clearly doesn't live here—and there *is* a touch in her of Jake Barnes's irony, when he says at the end of *The Sun Also Rises*, "Isn't it pretty to think so?" But only a touch. It never becomes anything as strong as bitterness. Indeed it seems to me that there is more to be said on the side of hearing these words as sincere for the moment at least, than there is on the side of interpreting them as wholly ironic, panicky, or deflationary.

William Lynch's thoughts about Christianity and comedy in *Christ and Apollo* are helpful in thinking about the effect of the wit in "Filling Station." Throughout Lynch's study of poetry and religion (published in 1960 and lacking any reference to Elizabeth Bishop), he is intent on making us hew to the world of time and sensation. Lynch emphasizes the *process* of living as necessary in our relationship with God, saying: "Time, even on the natural level, *is* a kind of ontological prayer. There is no other form of union with God. Ultimately the most solid form of prayer for the Christian, no matter what spiritual state he [or she] may be in (including that of high contemplation), is not rest but motion" (62).

Whatever one thinks about Lynch's overly emphatic argument, his presentation of the modern experience of religion is well adapted to Bishop's poetic practice and surprisingly apt for our own time as well, where, for example, he decries "the cheap strain of angel-ism" (109) in contemporary culture. The comedy of life as portrayed in literature, he suggests, is particularly characteristic of "the song of the indestructibility of the people," commenting further: "Rock-bottom being cannot be hurt. It is not the world of the clown. There is no sadness or self-pity in it" (107).

Elizabeth Bishop presents us with numerous working-class characters for whom these thoughts might be appropriate. One thinks of "Manuelzinho," "Helena Morley," Balthazár in "Twelfth Morning," "Squatter's Children," and "Pink Dog," some of whom we will consider in chapter 5. "Filling Station" is also about the working poor. However, its comedy is less sharp-edged, it seems to me, than that in some of these other works. In Lynch's terms it is therefore more purely comic. For Lynch, comedy's "whole function is to be a perpetual and funny, if disconcerting, reminder that it is the limited concrete that is the path to insight and salvation. Its whole art is to be an art of anamnesis, or memory, of the bloody human (in the sense in which the English use that adjective) as a path to God, or to any form of the great" (104).

In my reading of "Filling Station" these details about the "concrete" porch, humble and specific as they are, give rise to a perception of what it might feel like to live here: "Somebody loves us all."

Bishop didn't live here, of course, but she was capable of imaginatively (if briefly) entering a world where she could not linger. This is a poet's faculty and the reason that even a poem written by an unbeliever can be read as a religious text. What is the work of love, after all, even that which we are commanded to do by God? Isn't it always an activity of the mind and imagination? Seeing the world from someone else's perspective and rendering it as respectfully as we can, while always acknowledging that we are *not* the Other? In this regard, it is a form of what Rumi calls "Digging in the Ground."

An eye is meant to see things.
The soul is here for its own joy.
A head has one use: for loving a true love.
Legs to run after.

Love is for vanishing into the sky. The mind,
for learning what men have done and tried to do.
Mysteries are not to be solved. The eye goes blind
when it only wants to see *why*.

A lover is always accused of something.
But when he finds his love, whatever was lost
in the looking comes back completely changed.
On the way to Mecca, many dangers: thieves,
the blowing sand, only camel's milk to drink.
Still each pilgrim kisses the black stone there
with pure longing, feeling in the surface
the taste of the lips he wants.

This talk is like stamping new coins. They pile up,
while the real work is done outside
by someone digging in the ground. (*The Essential Rumi*, 107)

Mysteries Are Not to Be Solved

Of course, to place Rumi next to Elizabeth Bishop is to see how different they are as well as to see perhaps what they have in common. In one mood, Bishop called herself a "transcendentalist" by which I think she meant that the world of material reality (what Emerson called "nature") was full of meaning for her. She wasn't an ecstatic like Rumi, but she would have agreed that "Mysteries are not to be solved. The eye goes blind / when it only wants to see *why*." Digging in the ground produces its own meaning. For some of us this is a religious meaning, but for others it is meaningful without reference to something beyond itself. In Bishop's "Sandpiper," however, she records with some ruefulness the sandpiper's continual preoccupation with the stuff of nature.

> The world is a mist. And the world is
> minute and vast and clear. The tide
> is higher or lower. He couldn't tell you which.
> His beak is focussed; he is preoccupied,
>
> looking for something, something, something.
> Poor bird, he is obsessed!
> The millions of grains are black, white, tan, and gray,
> mixed with quartz grains, rose and amethyst. (*CP*, 131)

What one wants to say about this bird is that from one point of view he is missing the big picture. From another point of view, of course, he sees the subtleties invisible to others; he sees the rose and amethyst among the black, white, tan, and gray. Can we say which of these occupations is most in keeping with God's desires for us?

Bishop herself was the sandpiper, wondering if she was missing something but unable to keep from endlessly recording her most minute impressions, just like Robinson Crusoe in "Crusoe in England," dreaming of "infinities of islands": "knowing that I had to live / on each and every one, eventually, / for ages, registering their flora, / their fauna, their geography" (*CP*, 165). What a nightmare! Sometimes it is as well to let oneself be overcome by a sense of the whole.

But certainly it is human sometimes to be dry and destitute, to feel that each thing is only itself with nothing to bind one to another. Lynch speaks of this as "the equivocal mind," saying: "It is a mentality which believes that in the whole world of reality and being no two beings *are* in the same sense; everything is completely diverse from everything else." In this spirit, says Lynch, one comes to feel that "all is absurd, lonely, a private hell" (134). Elizabeth Bishop captures this feeling precisely when she speaks of "Everything only connected by 'and' and 'and' " (*CP*, 58).

This line occurs in Bishop's poem about the Bible, entitled "Over 2,000 Illustrations and a Complete Concordance." Like so many things in Bishop's work, however, this title is ambiguous, because it captures both what is missing from the book of life and what we wish we could find there: a world of individual experiences (illustrations) that *do* add up to something, where there is a "complete concordance" with some other level of reality and meaning. The fact that this title, with its allusion to the world of advertising, rings so hollowly only underscores the longing it addresses. Indeed the poem begins: "Thus *should* have been our travels: / serious, engravable" (My emphasis, *CP*, 57).

The poet/speaker is thinking about some books of her childhood, including a family Bible (still accessible in the Bishop archive in Nova Scotia) published in 1870 complete with Dr. William Smith's Complete Dictionary of the Bible and "embellished with over 2,000 Fine Scripture Illustrations." She is looking at them with the layered sight of a child who loves to look at pictures and of an adult who wishes she could find there more than is now available: "the human figure / far gone in history or theology, / gone with its camel or faithful horse." Gone where? One feels an absence of the real stuff of faith, something we could sink our teeth into. Bishop's Bible itself is serious, grim even (it contains no colored pictures), but the other books—she mentions in a letter *The Seven Wonders of the World* (*One Art*, 307)—contain images that are too highly colored. One remembers her mentioning "those unlovely gilded red and green books, filled with illustrations of the Bible stories" (*CPr*, 265) in her memoir, "In the Village." The world seems too pat, too sloppily rendered, in these pictures, which, after all, have no subtlety:

> Granted a page alone or a page made up
> of several scenes arranged in cattycornered rectangles
> or circles set on stippled gray,
> granted a grim lunette,
> caught in the toils of an initial letter,
> when dwelt upon, they all resolve themselves.
> The eye drops, weighted, through the lines
> the burin made, the lines that move apart
> like ripples above sand,
> dispersing storms, God's spreading fingerprint,
> and painfully, finally, that ignite
> in watery prismatic white-and-blue.

The language feels tangled and one must dwell on these words awhile before the sense of them emerges, even though one feels that there is something wonderful going on where "the eye drops" and the lines move apart "like ripples above sand" that become "God's spreading fingerprint."

Parallel to these lines that one stumbles over, the pictures are at first difficult to make out, but ultimately, she says, the message is clear, and it is one of lack. "When dwelt upon, they all resolve themselves" but into what? God's spreading fingerprint becomes unreadable in time, or what can be read—"painfully, finally"—is something not worth reading: "watery prismatic white-and-blue." Note that the poet has deliberately refused the opportunity for a rhyme in the last line, where, if she had written "watery prismatic blue and white," she would have given us a neat little couplet. Her purpose, however, seems to be to illustrate discordance, disillusionment: literally, the process of disengaging from pictures that are too neat or too easily resolved.

In the middle section of the poem, the poet recounts her travels in a way that makes them illustrations of "God's spreading fingerprint": each image moving away from the previous one so that there is no parallelism and no gestalt. Some of these travels surely recount Bishop's actual experience in North Africa where she encountered Islam and the Arab world. The images suggest various kinds of death, emotional and spiritual dryness, culminating with an image of the "whited sepulchre" of Matthew 23:27, except that even the "dead men's bones" that Jesus accuses hypocrites of concealing in hearts that are like "whitewashed tombs"—even these have disappeared.

> It was somewhere near there
> I saw what frightened me most of all:
> A holy grave, not looking particularly holy,
> one of a group under a keyhole-arched stone baldaquin
> open to every wind from the pink desert.
> An open, gritty, marble trough, carved solid
> with exhortation, yellowed
> as scattered cattle-teeth;
> half-filled with dust, not even the dust
> of the poor prophet paynim who once lay there.
> In a smart burnoose Khadour looked on amused. (*CP*, 58)

One notices the alienating language, words unfamiliar to the average English speaker such as baldaquin, paynim, burnoose; and who is Khadour? Yes, we can figure it out. There is an Arab guide in this picture, implicitly gesturing toward an empty tomb in the desert and enjoying the discomfiture of the Western tourists.

But everything in this scene resonates with the description of the biblical illustrations with which we began. Among those illustrations we have an Arab "with outstretched arm and hand" pointing to "the Tomb, the Pit, the Sepulcher" as though they were simply tired tourist attractions. (There *are* such pictures in the Bishop family Bible.) However, where the meanings projected by the illustrations were too emphatic and therefore unconvincing, *this* set of travel images recalls T. S. Eliot's "Waste Land" where meaning has been evacuated and replaced by figures who do not even wonder about what has been lost. The exhortations of a culture rooted in religious tradition have become merely decorations on the tomb of history. The *engravings* in the first section of the poem ("lines that move apart") are set side by side with the *grave*: "yellowed as scattered cattle-teeth." Even the ooh-ing sounds of "poor," "burnoose," "Khadour," "amused" suggest a dry wind blowing through the desert without end.

Lynch's characterization of the equivocal mind—"everything is absurd, lonely, a private hell"—is certainly relevant here. So it is no surprise when, after a stanza break, Bishop goes on: "Everything only connected by 'and' and 'and'." What is surprising, however, is what follows this line.

> Open the book. (The gilt rubs off the edges
> of the pages and pollinates the fingertips.)
> Open the heavy book. Why couldn't we have seen
> this old Nativity while we were at it?
> —the dark ajar, the rocks breathing with light,
> an undisturbed, unbreathing flame,
> colorless, sparkless, freely fed on straw,
> and, lulled within, a family with pets,
> —and looked and looked our infant sight away. (*CP*, 58–59)

INFANT SIGHT

The longing for meaning (and here specifically religious meaning) that was there all the time in the descriptions of the inadequacy of the merely human finally breaks through and announces itself in no uncertain terms. This picture is completely different from the colored illustrations with which she began. Also it must be said that there is no such picture in the Bulmer family Bible, so Bishop is going beyond the literal truth here. For me, the painter that repeatedly comes to mind is the Italian artist Giorgioni: "the dark ajar, the rocks breathing with light," as in Giorgione's "The Adoration of the Shepherds" perhaps. Bishop, a painter herself, often wrote in reaction to paintings. And what could be more quintessentially Bishop than the line: "And, lulled within, a family with pets," which is so funny and yet so heartbreaking at the same time? We feel the presence of the child and the child's longing in the adult who cannot get beyond what she calls here "infant sight," a literalness of the imagination. But, of course, there is so much more to be said about these lines than these few words. In a review of Bishop's work, reprinted in Schwartz and Estess's *Elizabeth Bishop and Her Art*, John Ashbery admitted that after twenty years he was "still unable to exhaust the meaning of that concluding line" (204).

We have spent a relatively large amount of time on "Over 2000 Illustrations and a Complete Concordance," but the purpose of doing so has been less to analyze Elizabeth Bishop's poem (which has been analyzed in greater detail by others) than to ponder the implications of reading poetry for a contemporary person of a religious cast of mind. The question here is in what sense are love and longing (the stuff of many poems) always, for a person of faith, exercises in approaching God. Jeanette Winterson and Rumi, an odd couple if there ever was one, suggest that they might be, and sometimes even in Elizabeth Bishop's poetry one sniffs in the salt air the absent sea.

Though she occasionally scoffed at mysticism (in parts of Simone Weil and Flannery O'Connor, for instance), Bishop's work is not entirely incongruous when set within a mystical context. St. Teresa's *Way of Perfection* and St. Ignatius's *Spiritual Exercises* have already made an appearance here as texts whose value Bishop openly acknowledged. In conjunction with St. Teresa one might also add St. John of the Cross, especially in connection with "The End of March" and "At the Fishhouses," which will be discussed in chapter 4.

At the vaguely Protestant Walnut Hill, where Bishop went to high school, not only did she write the mystical short story ("Into the Mountain"), she also, in all likelihood (since she was the editor), authored the unsigned editorial in "The Blue Pencil" (April 1930) that begins:

> All the ancient eremites, lost in visions we can neither see nor guess, have gone forever into their deserts and wildernesses. We cannot tell if they came at last to the land of their faith and desire. Neither have we the bright foreshadowings and ardent reflections of that land, that came to them in their rough caves and bare cells. Faith does not demand a martyrdom of us, but stern and remote she has turned away from us even her smile. With our insensitive ears it is useless to listen for music that has passed forever into the air, and fully as futile would be a search even for hints of all those older mysteries and raptures. Perhaps the saints and anchorites found their rewards in heaven, but there have been few for them here. For all their dreams and all their valiant prayers we have nothing left but interest and wonder. (Vassar Archive)

Though an early piece of writing, this captures perfectly Bishop's lifelong feeling of exclusion from religious mysteries and her "interest and wonder" in what they might have meant to those who could genuinely experience them.

In "Over 2000 Illustrations," opening the Bible pollinates the fingertips with gilt, which is both positive (fertile, golden) and negative (inducing guilt). We find Bishop in exactly the same frame of mind as the one reflected in the "Blue Pencil" editorial, asking the question: "Why couldn't we have seen / this old Nativity while we were at it?" Such a sight, precluded by our late modern sophistication, would have converted us: we would have been able to set ourselves aside "and looked and looked our infant sight away." Another way to read this line about "infant sight" is to see in it plenitude, the kind of spiritual vision of which Wordsworth wrote. To "look away," then, might take on the connotation of looking unreservedly, as in "go ahead. Look away." In any case, the use of *and* here has a totally different effect from "Everything only connected by 'and' and 'and.' " It seems to signal continuity and meaningfulness rather than sterile isolation, and thus it measures what we long for.

Certainly at times Love overcomes our sense of loss and fragmentation. In *The Cloud of Unknowing*, an anonymous mystical text from the fourteenth century, the so-called English author explores the function of contemplation in fulfilling what he (since he seems to have lived in a monastery, it was probably a he) calls "holy desire." In the highest form of contemplation, he tells us, our true being becomes paradoxically more apparent as it loses itself in God. This is what it might mean to look and look our infant sight away. "Nature designed the senses to acquire knowledge of the material world, not to understand the inner realities of the spirit." We come to an experience of fulfillment in the spirit only out of a sense of longing that is frustrated by all other forms of nourishment. "What I am trying to say is that man knows the things of the spirit more by what they are not than by what they are. When in reading or conversation we come upon things that our natural faculties cannot fathom, we may be sure that these are spiritual realities" (138–39).

Rainer Maria Rilke, in the second Duino Elegy, approaches the same set of ideas by means of artistic contemplation:

> Weren't you astonished by the caution of human gestures
> on Attic gravestones? Wasn't love and departure
> placed so gently on shoulders that it seemed to be made
> of a different substance than in our world? Remember the hands,
> how weightlessly they rest, though there is power in the torsos.
> These self-mastered figures know: "We can go this far,
> this is ours, to touch one another this lightly; the gods
> can press down harder upon us. But that is the gods' affair."
>
> If only we too could discover a pure, contained,
> human place, our own strip of fruit-bearing soil
> between river and rock. For our own heart always exceeds us,

as theirs did. And we can no longer follow it, gazing
into images that soothe it or into the godlike bodies
where, measured more greatly, it achieves a greater repose.

(Mitchell trans., 25–26)

In *The Book of Privy Counseling*, now published by Doubleday together
with *The Cloud of Unknowing*, the "English author" concludes:
"Knowledge is full of labor, but love, full of rest" (188). If at one time
certain visions could have allowed us to look and look our infant sight
away, they have mostly been replaced by the search for knowledge and
the active use of our faculties. In light of this, Bishop places words of
negation at the end of her poem: an "undisturbed, unbreathing"
flame, which is "colorless, sparkless" as though to suggest the idea of
the *apophatic*, that God is best known by negation as we are most
keenly aware of the spirit when our faculties are at rest. Another way
of saying this might be that mysteries are not to be solved but to be
registered, perhaps through poetry, "where, measured more greatly,
[they achieve] a greater repose."

4

SUFFERING MEANING

THE NATURE OF THINGS

If, unlike other forms of knowledge, the experience of God requires that we set aside our egos and all those faculties that feed them—reason, imagination, will, memory, perception—it will inevitably ring itself round with suffering. This is not to say that God demands that we suffer, only that, as we know It better, we inevitably experience a certain withdrawal from the contentments of being and that is painful. However, humans—as Geoffrey Hill once wrote—are dissatisfied *unless* we feel that there is something seriously at stake, something that hurts. In "Genesis," Hill insists: "By blood we live, the hot, the cold, / To ravage and redeem the world: / There is no bloodless myth will hold." We do seem to feel that suffering and meaning are conjoined, "Though Earth has rolled beneath her weight / The bones that cannot bear the light" (5).

In our old friend *The Cloud of Unknowing*, the English author warns us against imagining that contemplation will make us happy in any common way, and in this respect he is as intentionally discouraging as any contemporary critic of New Age panaceas, insisting that perfect correspondence to God's special grace "consists in a strong, deep, interior sorrow." And then he tells us what he means by this: "he alone understands the deep universal reason for sorrow who experiences *that he is*. Every other motive pales beside this one. He alone feels authentic sorrow who realizes not only *what he is* but *that he is*. Anyone who has not felt this should really weep, for he has never experienced real sorrow" (103).

Now if we go back to the end of Bishop's story "The Country Mouse," we can see that it becomes a lot clearer when it is understood in connection with this passage from the English author. For, leaving aside for the moment "In the Waiting Room" where she transforms this experience into a poem, in her prose piece Bishop says: "A feeling of absolute and utter desolation came over me. I felt . . . *myself*. In a few days it would be my seventh birthday. I felt *I, I, I*, and looked at the three strangers in panic. I was *one* of them, too, inside my scabby body and wheezing lungs. 'You're in for it now,' something said. . . . *Why* was I a human being?" (*CPr*, 32–33). She is not, it turns out, bemoaning her particular failings. Although she mentions her "scabby body and wheezing lungs," it is not these attributes that frighten her but instead the simple fact of being, being a human, which in its individuality implies an immense space of non-being, of Otherness, a situation not unlike that which she expresses with the line: "Everything only connected by 'and' and 'and.' "

Suffering meaning cannot, it seems, be disengaged from suffering limitation, and at some level it may be that the experience of meaning itself cannot be disengaged from suffering. I want to begin here with a poem by Emily Dickinson that seems to me to be about this matter. It is a puzzling poem as perhaps it should be, given such a peculiar subject.

> There's a certain Slant of light,
> Winter Afternoons"—
> That oppresses, like the Heft
> Of Cathedral Tunes—
>
> Heavenly Hurt, it gives us—
> We can find no scar,
> But internal difference—
> Where the Meanings, are—
>
> None may teach it — Any—
> 'Tis the seal Despair—
> An imperial affliction
> Sent us of the Air—
>
> When it comes, the Landscape listens—
> Shadows — hold their breath—
> When it goes, 'tis like the Distance
> On the look of Death — (Johnson #320)

What is this poem about? A beam of light? Hymns, or music more generally? Does the first line—"There's a certain Slant of light"—actually establish the subject of the poem (as light) or is it a metaphor for something else, for something that elsewhere Dickinson calls "that white sustenance, Despair"?

Or perhaps this poem is not about despair after all, but about something that might produce despair. About being penetrated by the overwhelming sensation of differing and deferral itself, what the French call *différance?* "Everything only connected by 'and' and 'and'."

The poem is set in winter, in the bleakest season of the year in Dickinson's Massachusetts. Light is slanting downward and the spirit is oppressed, as it is by the weight (heft) of certain kinds of church music. But then the poet says: "Heavenly hurt it gives us." This feeling of oppression (and depression, which is a secondary meaning of "oppression") is not just a mood, an emotion. We are being knocked around by something or by someone. Someone who seems completely inaccessible in this poem and yet who is all around us, in the very air we breathe. The suffering we experience in this instance is called a "Heavenly hurt," which we might interpret in two ways as (1) coming from Heaven (thus, of God), and (2) heaving us (the present tense of *heft*) up to heaven, elevating us, as certain kinds of music (I think of Messaien) may be experienced as simultaneously oppressive and uplifting.

The second stanza is the one in which this notion of "suffering meaning" is most explicitly addressed. Though we are hurt by this sense of things (whatever can be conveyed by a certain kind of light or music) "we can find no scar / but internal difference— / where the meanings, are." Nothing external has changed, it seems, and that is why one feels that Dickinson is not speaking here about death *as an event* but rather more generally about a realization of the nature of things, that "in the midst of life, we are in death." What does it mean to be embodied? What does it mean to exist? What is the true nature of the Real?

In *The Perennial Philosophy*, Aldous Huxley talks about the way suffering comes with the territory of being human. According to Huxley, who is speaking in his mystical voice in this volume, suffering arises from separation and individuation. "The capacity to suffer arises where there is imperfection, disunity, and separation from an embracing totality; and the capacity is actualised to the extent that imperfection, disunity, and separateness are accompanied by an urge towards an intensification of these creaturely conditions" (234). It may sound at times as though Huxley believes that we can overcome this suffering by simply "choosing selflessness," but actually he says such suffering "is a necessary part of creatureliness. In so far as this is the case, creation is the beginning of the Fall" (235).

Meaning, of course, is an aspect of individuation and separateness. It positions itself against something else, non-meaning, and as such its very content is an acknowledgment of grief and loss. In some mystical traditions, in Buddhism, for instance, or Christian Negative Theology, one merges with God only at the expense of everything else because God is no-thing. In mystical ecstasy there is no self, no world, no truth, no time, no extent, and so on. No separation, therefore no being. Most of us haven't been there, but if we are particularly sensitive or philosophical, like Elizabeth Bishop and Emily Dickinson, we may experience Being (where there *is* world, self, and time) as separateness from God, or as being alone.

However, what I am trying to get at here is a very different matter from the isolated human subject whose assertion of will and striving may be thought to give life meaning in the face of the failure of transcendence. We are not talking about the "existential self" here but about something closer to what late modern Continental philosophy—in the work of such people as Jacques Derrida and Maurice Blanchot—has identified as the human condition, the condition of un-representability. In this orientation, writing itself is always what Blanchot calls writing toward "the disaster," the prior condition of absolute loss that cannot be written. As Thomas Carlson explains the relation between Negative Theology and Poststructuralism: "In Blanchot and Derrida alike a basic premise of all apophatic theology would seem to apply also to a basic dilemma of mortal discourse: both move toward that which they cannot reach" (169), God, Death, the Real.

From this perspective, death, like God, interrupts our claims to knowledge, not just in Time but in effect. All that which we cannot know (not just what we do not know) is necessary to us, and since we exist "in denial," as it were, since we are refused this knowledge, we are tormented by a heavenly hurt the recognition of which is what I am calling here "suffering meaning." Dickinson tells us that it cannot be taught: "None may teach it Any / 'Tis the seal Despair."

If one has felt it, as Bishop describes feeling it at the extremely early age of seven, things shift their ground. The term "realization" seems appropriate here because something has been understood (realized) but also "the landscape listens. / Shadows hold their breath." The world of "reality" becomes sharper, clearer, more distinctly painful and at the same time more *unreal* or surreal. One cannot communicate the sense of what has been lost. "When it goes 'tis like the Distance / On the look of death." In the aftermath of this piercing perception, we find ourselves gazing on nothing, the face of our own exile.

Why might the poet believe that there is a purpose behind this "Imperial affliction / sent us of the Air"? Derrida was loath to speak of such a purpose, as he was loath to speak of God, except as a hypothetical limit. Contemplatives also experience this sense of negation, however, and for them its purpose is literally crucial, of the cross.

THE DARK NIGHT OF THE SOUL

In "Desolation as Dark Night: The Transformative Influence of Wisdom in John of the Cross," Constance Fitzgerald spells out the purpose of suffering meaning and meaning as suffering in the work of the Spanish mystic. Referencing John's *Living Flame of Love* (3:19–22), Fitzgerald says: "Only when we become aware of our emptiness, in the face of the experience of the fragility and breakdown of what or whom we have staked our lives on, the limitation and failure of our life project and life love, the shattering of our dreams and meanings, can the depths of thirst and hunger that exist in the human person, the infinite capacity [for God], really be felt" (98). For Fitzgerald, who lives a contemplative life in a Carmelite monastery in Baltimore, there are times when devotion to Jesus as Wisdom "takes on all the marks of crucifixion: suffering, isolation, failure, marginality, rejection, abandonment, hopelessness, meaninglessness, death" (101).

For the person of faith this can be excruciating, because it is felt as a door being slammed not simply by a perception of "the nature of things" (Bishop's desolation) but by the very being to whom one has devoted one's life. Fitzgerald is very clear about this: "Dark Night is not primarily *some thing*, an impersonal darkness like a difficult situation or distressful psychological condition, but *someone*, a presence leaving an indelible imprint on the human spirit and consequently on one's entire life" (101). As such, it is an "Imperial affliction / sent us of the Air."

The so-called Dark Sonnets of Gerard Manley Hopkins are memorable poems of affliction that give voice to the dark night of the soul. I will include only one of them here, but there are others that are equally powerful. This one, however, is particularly useful for our purposes because it connects the experience of affliction with the experience of selfhood, Bishop's horror of "*I, I, I.*"

> I wake and feel the fell of dark, not day.
> What hours, O what black hours we have spent
> This night! what sights you, heart, saw; ways you went!
> And more must, in yet longer light's delay.
>
> With witness I speak this. But where I say
> Hours I mean years, mean life. And my lament
> Is cries countless, cries like dead letters sent
> To dearest him that lives alas! away.

> I am gall, I am heartburn. God's most deep decree
> Bitter would have me taste: my taste was me;
> Bones built in me, flesh filled, blood brimmed the curse.
> Selfyeast of spirit a dull dough sours. I see
> The lost are like this, and their scourge to be
> As I am mine, their sweating selves; but worse. (130–31)

I have read this poem for so many years (beginning when I was an undergraduate searching for a senior thesis topic) that it is difficult for me to remember how I stumbled over Hopkins's lines the first time, uncertain how to read this clotted syntax, how to take in these gouts of spiritual gore. Reading the poem slowly out loud helps one place the stresses where they should go, which is often in packs of two or more, what Hopkins called "sprung rhythm": "*Bones built* in me, *flesh filled, blood brimmed* the *curse.*" This takes the absolutely regular iambic pentameter, the common English meter, of the first line— "I *wake* and *feel* the *fell* of *dark*, not *day*"—and hardens it into a dagger or a gnarled root. In the most agonized moments of the poem, almost everything is stressed: "*cries countless, cries* like *dead letters sent.*" And, of course, it must be said that this is also an insomnia poem, like Bishop's "Insomnia" discussed in chapter 3.

Hopkins was an English Catholic, a Jesuit, but his dark sonnets are often linked to the works of St. John of the Cross, the sixteenth-century Spanish monk who, along with St. Teresa of Avila, founded the Carmelite Order. In Volume II of *The Dark Night of the Soul* (3:3), John says:

> God strips [the advanced soul] of powers and affections and senses, spiritual as well as sensual, interior as well as exterior, leaving the mind in darkness, and the will dried up, and the memory empty, and the desires of the soul in deep distress, bitterness, and oppression, depriving it of the sense and pleasure which it had previously enjoyed from these spiritual blessings. (52)

Why should one have to endure this, one might ask? The answer in apophatic (negative) theology is in order that we be moved away from things into no-thing, where unity with the godhead comes at the price of control and representation, denying us the graspable, the tenable, the repeatable.

However, there is an activity that we must carry on during the dark night of the soul and that activity is faith, what Fitzgerald calls "a free, trustful commitment to the impossible." We must accept suffering in the interest of a meaning that we cannot grasp. "Overcoming the will to die, this love lives honestly with the pain of its own woundedness and longing." For John of the Cross, the pursuit of knowledge is replaced by the operations of Sophia (or Wisdom). "This subversive dynamic of beloved Sophia is set in motion when human suffering, loss and emptiness have reached such a pitch of consciousness, . . . that the capacity of the human person is hollowed out for deeper knowing, deeper mutuality" (Fitzgerald, 105).

Hopkins is the English-language poet who most effectively captures the soul's agonized sense of abandonment where, for example, he speaks of "cries like dead letters sent / To dearest him who lives alas! away." Surely these dead letters are prayers, suggesting the ongoing operations of faith in the midst of torment.

Elizabeth Bishop, too, knew the dark night of the soul, but when the great love of her life, Lota de Macedo Soares, died, Bishop turned not to Hopkins (though she had read him appreciatively for many years) but to George Herbert, who she said was the only poet she could bear to read. Herbert is ultimately more reassuring than Hopkins, but even Herbert's work is rife with references to spiritual affliction. He wrote five poems with the title "Affliction," one of which contains the memorable line, "My thoughts are all a case of knives," a line Bishop quotes in her early poem "Wading At Wellfleet."

Probably the most Hopkins-like poem Herbert wrote, however, was not an affliction poem but, interestingly, "Prayer (I)," where in a single sonnet he captures the whole life of the soul in its pilgrimage toward God, culminating with the idea of meaning as emerging out of the process of suffering.

> Prayer the Church's banquet, Angels age,
>   God's breath in man returning to his birth,
>   The soul in paraphrase, heart in pilgrimage,
> The Christian plummet sounding heav'n and earth;
> Engine against th'Almighty, sinner's tower,
>   Reversed thunder, Christ-side-piercing spear,
>   The six-days world transposing in an hour,
> A kind of tune, which all things hear and fear;
> Softness, and peace, and joy, and love, and bliss,
>   Exalted Manna, gladness of the best,
>   Heaven in ordinary, man well dressed,
> The Milky Way, the bird of Paradise,
>   Church-bells beyond the stars heard, the soul's blood,
>   The land of spices; something understood. (45–46)

In the life of prayer, this poem says, the soul will inevitably experience rebellion against God. Herbert calls this "Engine against th'Almighty," a function of human pride (the "sinner's tower"). We therefore become one with those who crucified Christ, but we are also ourselves afflicted, feeling Christ's "side-piercing spear." Herbert puts his poetic finger on the way suffering meaning undoes our whole sense of things for a time ("the six-days world transposing in an hour"). He also uses the same image as Emily Dickinson where he speaks of "A kind of *tune* that all things hear and fear." Her slant of light is like his plummet "sounding heaven and earth."

Yet for George Herbert, as for Constance Fitzgerald, there is what Bishop calls in her poem "Roosters": "inescapable hope, the pivot." Herbert's language here gives us "the roll, the rise, the carol, the creation" of lyric poetry in such phrases as "Church-bells beyond the stars heard, the soul's blood," a line as full of sprung rhythm as anything in Hopkins himself but also full of rainbows. Suffering meaning can mean suffering a sense of rejection and isolation, but it has a different resonance when knowledge is replaced by Sophia or Wisdom. Then suffering meaning *becomes* us as it becomes God, an exaltation.

THE END OF THE ROAD

In light of this trajectory, I want to examine a poem by Elizabeth Bishop that is not as firmly located within religious crisis as those of Hopkins or Herbert and yet suggests them both. The poem is called "The End of March." It begins with a landscape of misery that is eminently recognizable in this context.

> It was cold and windy, scarcely the day
> to take a walk on that long beach.
> Everything was withdrawn as far as possible,
> indrawn: the tide far out, the ocean shrunken,
> sea birds in ones or twos.
> The rackety, icy, offshore wind
> numbed our faces on one side;
> disrupted the formation
> of a lone flight of Canada geese;
> and blew back the low, inaudible rollers
> in upright, steely mist. (*CP*, 179–80)

Encountering this first stanza, it is hard for a reader of poetry *not* to think of Matthew Arnold's "Dover Beach" where the beach scene sets forth the prospect of the loss of God in the modern world, especially where Bishop says: "Everything was withdrawn as far as possible, / indrawn: the tide far out, the ocean shrunken." In Arnold's late-nineteenth-century poem, once a set piece in many a schoolroom, he addresses the death of God by saying:

> The sea of faith
> Was once, too, at the full, and round earth's shore
> Lay like the folds of a bright girdle furled;
> But now I only hear
> Its melancholy, long, *withdrawing* roar,
> Retreating to the breath
> Of the night-wind down the vast edges drear
> And naked shingles of the world.
>
> (Warren and Erskine, 447, emphasis mine)

In Bishop's poem too the emotional content of the first stanza is spiritual desolation. Though the speaker is taking a walk, there is more of a sense of lack of progression than of progress, as, when one walks in a vast landscape, the horizon endlessly recedes and one feels, often, lonely, embattled, without adequate means to advance, an isolate speck drawing no nearer to "what there is." The voice of the waves is "inaudible." The winds frustrate effort, disrupting forward movement in the "lone flight" of the Canada geese, in the waves, in the lengths of the lines that are pulled in, becoming noticeably shorter as the stanza proceeds. The "upright steely mist" produced by frustration is emotionally correlated to the figures who have steeled themselves for this walk against the wind where the small globes of water might also be seen as tears, or rather as the dispersal of tears across a broad landscape, not raining down in fertile expression but refined into a sense of steely display. And she goes on:

> The sky was darker than the water.
> —*it* was the color of mutton-fat jade.
> Along the wet sand, in rubber boots, we followed
> a track of big dog-prints (so big
> they were more like lion-prints). Then we came on
> lengths and lengths, endless, of wet white string,
> looping up to the tide-line, down to the water,
> over and over. Finally, they did end:
> a thick white snarl, man-size, awash,
> rising on every wave, a sodden ghost,
> falling back, sodden, giving up the ghost. . . .
> A kite string?—But no kite.

This section seems to me to make a particularly strong allusion to the Dark Sonnets of Gerard Manley Hopkins, especially in the phrase "lengths and lengths, endless," which is so like Hopkins' "No Worst, There Is None" where he moans: "O the mind, mind has mountains, cliffs of fall, / frightful" (127). The "sodden ghost" calls to mind "the sodden-with-its-sorrowing heart" of Hopkins' "Wreck of the Deutschland" (27). It is the end of March, the end of the long march, or, as Robert Lowell puts it in "Quaker Graveyard in Nantucket" (another poem about spiritual desolation and one of Bishop's favorites), "This is the end of running on the waves; / We are poured out like water" (17).

In the midsection of Bishop's poem, she imagines entering a "crooked box / set up on pilings"—"my proto-dream-house, / my crypto-dream-house," she calls it—an actual abandoned structure in Duxbury, but for her a place that at first seems to offer shelter and conventual solitude. "I'd like to retire there and do *nothing*, / or nothing much, forever, in two bare rooms: / look through binoculars, read boring books, / old, long, long, books, and write down useless notes" just like her narrator in the much earlier story "In Prison." The *grog à l'américaine* that she imagines drinking (reminiscent of the drunken beachcomber in "The Sea & The Shore"), with its "lovely diaphanous blue flame" provides an intoxicating fantasy, momentarily evoking the "living flame of love" of St. John of the Cross as an alternative to the dark night of the soul.

But Bishop is more the poet of suffering here than the one who experiences exaltation.

> A light to read by—perfect! But—impossible.
> And that day the wind was much too cold
> even to get that far,
> and of course the house was boarded up.

The voice of George Herbert, if one hears it at all, is audible not in this midsection of the poem but in the last stanza, where, as in many poems by Herbert, the spiritual temperature finally warms a bit and the sun makes an appearance.

> On the way back our faces froze on the other side.
> The sun came out for just a minute.
> For just a minute, set in their bezels of sand,
> the drab, damp, scattered stones
> were multi-colored,
> and all those high enough threw out long shadows,
> individual shadows, then pulled them in again.
> They could have been teasing the lion sun,

except that now he was behind them
—a sun who'd walked the beach the last low tide,
making those big, majestic paw-prints,
who perhaps had batted a kite out of the sky to play with.

The return of the sun is, of course, a form of grace that creates a moment of illumination in which "the drab, damp, scattered stones" become multicolored. We know the poet's imagination has been released into a different kind of interpretation than before, one full of laughter and metaphor, because she tells us that it is not so much the outside world that has changed but rather her own relationship to it. When the rocks throw out their shadows and pull them in again, she no longer interprets this as a sign of destitution. Instead she says: "They could have been teasing the lion sun."

It may occur to one at this point that the end of March is also the season of Passover, and in Christianity the time when Good Friday is followed by Easter and the resurrection. J. D. McClatchy mentions that the "mutton-fat jade" might evoke the paschal lamb. Both the lion and the sun are sometimes symbols of Christ, the lion of Judah. (The lion as Christ appears in Marianne Moore's "In Distrust of Merits," which we know Bishop admired: "O black imperial lion / of the Lord—emblem / of a risen world," 136.) In Bishop's personification of the sun, she coyly invites us to think of the Son: "except that now he was behind them / —a sun who'd walked the beach the last low tide" and brought redemption, "making those big, majestic paw-prints (like Augustine's reference to the footprints of God in Book XI, Chapter 28, of *The City of God*, a work we know Bishop was reading)." The lion is sometimes a symbol of recurring spiritual struggle, and, in its general association with devouring, it can also be associated with the special symbolism of Time.

But this is a playful god "who perhaps had batted a kite out of the sky to play with," and is therefore more like Herbert's God than like Hopkins's. In many mystical traditions, of course, God is playful and the saint is also a fool. "The End of March" suggests that "suffering meaning" may take on various colorations of the spirit, even motley. The lengths of wet white string ("man-size") are an enigma that says more about us, perhaps, than about God.

A COMIC INTERLUDE

Can suffering meaning be comic as well as tragic? Some writers answer in the affirmative. For example, the Presbyterian theologian Frederick

Buechner has written a series of novels (one called, interestingly enough, *Lion Country*) around the comic saint and sage Leo Bebb, whose saintliness is very peculiar, even at times absurd. Then again in Flannery O'Connor, though the characters rarely laugh, we, her readers, who are "suffering meaning" along with such folks as Mrs. Turpin and Obadiah Elihu Parker, often do. This brings me to the following contemporary poem by Kathleen Norris where we find an image of Christ as a figure who might have batted a kite out of the sky to play with.

> He is there, like Clouseau,
> at the odd moment,
> just right: when he climbs
> out of the fish pond
> into which he has spectacularly
> fallen, and says condescendingly
> to his hosts, the owners
> of the estate, "I fail
> where others succeed." You know
> this is the truth. You know
> he'll solve the mystery,
>
> unprepossessing
> as he is, the last
> of the great detectives.
> He'll blend again into the scenery, and
> more than once, be taken
> for the gardener. "Come
> now," he says, taking us
> for all we're worth: "sit
> in the low place."
> Why not! We ask, so easy
> to fall for a man
> who makes us laugh. "Invite those
> you do not know, people
> you'd hardly notice." He puts
> us on, we put him on; another
> of his jokes. "There's
> room," he says. The meal is
> good, absurdly
> salty, but delicious. Charlie
> Chaplin put it this way: "I want to play
> the role of Jesus. I look the part.
> I'm a Jew.
> And I'm a comedian." (Impasto, 179–80)

The title of this poem is "Luke 14: A Commentary." In it, Norris is having fun with several parables that appear in that chapter including the one where Christ tells the banquet guests that it is better to take "the low place"; another where the master's invitation is rejected by his guests and he therefore sends his servants into the street to invite the hoi polloi; and a third about salt: "Salt is good; but if salt has lost its taste, how shall its saltiness be restored? It is fit neither for the land nor for the dunghill; men throw it away. He who has ears to hear, let him hear."

Of course, Norris also has a serious purpose in writing this poem, and her puns lean in that direction: "He puts / us on, we put him on; another / of his jokes." Luke 14 is one of those difficult chapters in the New Testament that has worried Christians for centuries, because in it Christ says: "If anyone comes to me and does not hate his own father and mother and wife and children and brothers and sisters, yes, and even his own life, he cannot be my disciple." Who would want to follow such a messiah?

In Norris's poem, however, we should want to follow him. Though his language is "absurdly salty," the meal is delicious. Only by failing where others succeed, only by putting us on and "taking us / for all we are worth," can he preserve what otherwise would be lost. "You know / this is truth. You know / he'll solve the mystery." Only by putting us on can he make us put Him on, as Paul recommends in I Corinthians 15:54 and in Romans 13:12. Suffering is a part of this process. As is laughter, perhaps.

AT THE FISHHOUSES

Suffering and humor also make an appearance in Elizabeth Bishop's great poem "At the Fishhouses," arguably the most serious poem she wrote about "suffering meaning" and yet one that inevitably makes audiences laugh. One can hear their laughter in the recording of Bishop reading her own poems, recently rereleased by Random House. The doubleness of the poem is something that readers often struggle with. Guy Rotella, for example, claims that in part the poem "prepares [us] for revelation *and* suggests that any vision is humanly imposed on the natural scene" (221).

Though acknowledging its doubleness, I want to depart from the usual demurrers and suggest a reading of the poem that doesn't dissolve into skepticism. This will take us into some discussion of Wisdom as understood in Pre-Christian Judaism. The poem begins with an old man, a figure so archetypal, despite the specific details of his activities, that he inevitably assumes a kind of mythic significance.

> Although it is a cold evening,
> down by one of the fishhouses
> an old man sits netting,
> his net, in the gloaming almost invisible,
> a dark purple-brown,
> and his shuttle worn and polished. (*CP*, 64–66)

The tone is muted, the scene a bit reminiscent of Rembrandt in his later years, the figure finely etched but at the same time making reference to something offstage, something "almost invisible," looming like Death. His shuttle is worn and polished. Time seems to be destructive but also instructive in the case of the old man, who has witnessed "the decline in the population" but who has also learned to use his time effectively "while he waits for a herring boat to come in."

In discussing this poem, Thomas Travisano speaks of "traces of sublimity," saying, "Time's signature on this place is ambiguous. Marked by losses, weathered by age, undermined by uncertainties, the setting can still be seen as imbued with an indefinable nobility as well as sadness" (124). In the long initial section describing the old man and his Canadian setting, there is a kind of stateliness in the language that requires us to slow down as we read it, to slow down and to defer to it, withdrawing our egos and their urgency to "get to the point." We'll get there, but not before we have learned to sit quietly and pay attention.

> All is silver: the heavy surface of the sea,
> swelling slowly as if considering spilling over,
> is opaque, but the silver of the benches,
> the lobster pot, and masts, scattered
> among the wild jagged rocks,
> is of an apparent translucence
> like the small old buildings with an emerald moss
> growing on their shoreward walls.

It might be a Romantic landscape with its "wild, jagged rocks," except for the strategies Bishop uses to foil our Romantic inclinations: that is, the stink of codfish so strong "it makes one's nose run and one's eyes water"; the beautiful, iridescent herring scales "with small iridescent flies crawling on them"; the old man himself who "accepts a Lucky Strike" and seems to prefer to speak not of the glorious (or affectionate) past but "of codfish and herring."

There are a lot of references to verticality: the gangplanks "slant up," the wheelbarrows can "be pushed up and down" on them, the sea is swelling up, the population is going down, and, most arrestingly:

> *Up* on the little slope behind the houses,
> set in the sparse bright sprinkle of grass,
> is an ancient wooden capstan,
> cracked, with two long bleached wooden handles
> and some melancholy stains, like dried blood,
> where the ironwork has rusted. (My emphasis)

A *capstan* is a vertical cylinder used for hoisting weights by winding in a cable. Why all this verticality? Why, oh why, this disassembled cross with its "melancholy stains, like dried blood"? Why, in the second half of the poem, do we find "back, behind us," behind us and *up*, a million Christmas trees standing, "waiting for Christmas." Are we, too, like Simone Weil "waiting for God"? Too serious, you say? Too insistent on the religious symbolism? Well, we are soon to find relief.

In the meantime we must go down and immerse ourselves in the destructive element. Bishop inserts a hinge stanza to take us from the land into the sea, a stanza that makes us fully aware that we are descending and that descent—because it is given such time and attention in the poem—will be significant.

> Down at the water's edge, at the place
> where they haul up the boats, up the long ramp
> descending into the water, thin silver
> tree trucks are laid horizontally
> across the gray stones, down and down
> at intervals of four or five feet.

One long sentence, taking us "down and down," into the water.

Then the cello-ist second part of the poem begins, with "Cold dark deep and absolutely clear, / element bearable to no mortal, / to fish and to seals . . . ." Travisano speaks of the "incantatory magnificence" of the language, but at the beginning of the section, it trails off. The water is too cold. We must have something warmer in the way of comic relief.

> One seal particularly
> I have seen here evening after evening.
> He was curious about me. He was interested in music;
> like me a believer in total immersion,
> so I used to sing him Baptist hymns.

> I also sang "A Mighty Fortress Is Our God."
> He stood up in the water and regarded me
> steadily, moving his head a little.
> Then he would disappear, then suddenly emerge
> almost in the same spot, with a sort of shrug
> as if it were against his better judgment.

Now, in addition to being delightfully realistic, this seal seems to me to be a figure for Bishop herself, who like the seal is humorously said to be "a believer in total immersion." By making the religious reference here so overt, Bishop is disclaiming the heaviness of discourse about God. But the peek-a-boo game that the seal is playing is very much like what is happening in the poem itself, with Bishop inviting us to think of Christian meanings, then backing off, then reappearing again "almost in the same spot, with a sort of shrug / as if it were against [her] better judgment."

The same spot is what we return to after the comic interlude—the same words with which we began this section, followed by something different:

> Cold dark deep and absolutely clear,
> the clear gray icy water . . .

She breaks off again, and here is where we get the Christmas trees.

> Back behind us,
> the tall dignified firs begin.
> Bluish, associating with their shadows,
> a million Christmas trees stand
> waiting for Christmas.

We, too, Bishop's readers, are waiting for something, something meaningful, something that is perhaps unrepresentable, ungraspable, lost in those ellipses that twice follow the attempt to specify what is there in the "cold dark deep and absolutely clear" element, something under erasure.

But the poet must speak. And finally she does, and we find that the waiting has after all been worthwhile, for the language at last attains what Seamus Heaney has called "that *sine qua non* of all lyric utterance, a completely persuasive inner cadence which is deeply intimate with the laden water of full tide" (106). After a suspension, we catch the momentum of the last lines and are finally able to ride it all the way in, beginning with:

> The water seems suspended
> above the rounded gray and blue-gray stones.
> I have seen it over and over, the same sea, the same,
> slightly, indifferently swinging above the stones,
> icily free above the stones,
> above the stones and then the world.

Notice how she keeps starting over—above the stones, over and over, the same sea, the same—until finally there is a sudden lift: "above the stones and then the world." This sudden lift, it seems, allows her to go forward now without stopping.

> If you would dip your hand in,
> your wrist would ache immediately
> your bones would begin to ache and your hand would burn
> as if the water were a transmutation of fire
> that feeds on stones and burns with a dark gray flame.

The language becomes that of mystical theology.

> If you tasted it, it would first taste bitter,
> then briny, then surely burn your tongue.

Isn't this the essence of suffering meaning, the coal applied to the lips of Isaiah?

> It is like what we imagine knowledge to be:
> dark, salt, clear, moving, utterly free,

Notice that now we have commas dividing these adjectives, each only itself, "utterly free," and in motion:

> drawn from the cold hard mouth
> of the world, derived from the rocky breasts
> forever, flowing and drawn, and since
> our knowledge is historical, flowing, and flown.

It is true that Bishop says this knowledge is drawn from the "cold hard mouth *of the world*," not of God. But that doesn't mean that it is not, in another sense, *of* God. What kind of knowledge are we talking

about here, after all? It isn't knowledge whose only source and refer-
ent is sensory experience, because we know that the sea from which it
comes is "above the stones and then the world." In fact, it is clear that
we cannot *understand* this knowledge, for if we try to investigate it, it
will burn us "as if the water were a transmutation of fire / that feeds
on stones and burns with a dark gray flame." Bishop deliberately
confuses the senses here: water is transmuted into fire and later into a
kind of milk, reminding one of St. Teresa's *Way of Perfection* where
she speaks of the soul as being like an infant at its mother's breast,
receiving God's truth (Sophia) without any conscious effort on its
part as a kind of milk (205).

With its female inflection, this knowledge "derived from the rocky
breasts" of experience inevitably summons up the figure of Sophia.
Constance Fitzgerald's essay on St. John of the Cross presents him as
deeply influenced by the Pre-Christian Judaic Wisdom traditions, and
John of the Cross, as well as other mystics, certainly comes to mind as
one reads this poem. Fitzgerald claims: "The biblical depiction of
Wisdom is invariably female, suggesting a person rather than a concept or an attribute. Biblical Wisdom is treated not as an 'it' but as
a summoning 'I,' a 'sister, mother, female beloved' " (107), someone
with breasts but also a figure whose presence implies the connection
between knowledge and human suffering, the dark night of the soul.

Bishop does not speak of what this knowledge is because it is
ineffable. All one can say is that this element—"bearable to no mortal, /
to fish and to seals"—is "*like* what we imagine knowledge to be." Like
the truth that becomes present in mystical experiences, we draw it
from the world's rocky breasts if we can. But we cannot retain it. In
addition to being ineffable, it is ephemeral, "flowing, and flown."

We might profitably go back to William Lynch here and to Bishop's
comment about the poet's relation to poetic truth: "The target is a
moving target and the marksman is also moving" (Schwartz and Estess,
275). Lynch, who is writing about poetry and religion in *Christ and
Apollo*, insists that we cannot know God except in the midst of life.
"Time, even on the natural level, *is* a kind of ontological prayer. There
is no other form of union with God." For him, the fish is a perfect
symbol of the soul because "it must breathe its air (the infinite) through
the water (the finite)" (86). Now we can see better why so much of the
poem is about time and verticality, moving us down and then up.
"Ultimately the most solid form of prayer for the Christian, no matter
what spiritual state he [or she] may be in (including that of high contemplation), is not rest but motion" (62). This is why, for Lynch,
poetry can be (is) such an important medium of religious meditation.

That "At the Fishhouses" does not try to give us the substance of spiritual meaning is partly its point. What it does give us is a set of analogues or allusions to the experience of suffering meaning, analogues and allusions that confess their distance from their object (knowledge, truth) even as they point to it. The painful clarity of this experience of fullness and loss is comparable to what George Herbert calls "something understood," but for Bishop here as for the mystics elsewhere it is not a "thing" at all because it is ungraspable. "The spiritual does not present itself as a tenable substance but, rather, through its absence," according to Emmanuel Levinas (Jarraway, 138). "When it comes," Emily Dickinson says, "the landscape listens. / Shadows hold their breath," waiting like Bishop's Christmas trees, "associating with their shadows." When it goes, as it does here, as it must do in our lives,

> 'tis like the distance
> —on the look of death.

5

BLESSED ARE THE POOR

UNREASONABLE CHARITY

The charge often made against mysticism is that it concentrates wholly on the individual's relationship with God, thereby assuming a passive relation to injustice. What about our commitment to others, such critics ask; what about the injunction to "do justice and love kindness" as it says in Micah (6:8)? With justice comes the question of earthly rewards and those who are excluded from them, in other words "the poor," by which, it seems, we are meant to understand not simply those who lack wealth but many others as well.

The Bible is full of talk about the poor in both the Old and the New Testaments. In Matthew (5:3) the "poor in spirit" are blessed, "for theirs is the kingdom of heaven." In Luke (6:20) Jesus looks upon his disciples and says: "Blessed be ye poor, for yours is the realm of God," and further down, "But woe unto you that are rich! For ye have received your consolation" (24). Though the poor in both the Hebrew Scriptures and the Gospels are regarded as a perennial problem in society ("The poor you have always with you," Matt. 26:11), this very fact is cause for charity in Deuteronomy: "For the poor shall never cease out of the land: *therefore* I command thee, saying, Thou shalt open thine hand wide unto thy brother, to thy poor, and to thy needy, in thy land" (11). Everywhere in the Bible the faithful are enjoined to be kind to those who are needy. Why then are some who profess to be Christians so hard-hearted (and tightfisted) when it comes to the needs of "the poor"? Perhaps the answer is they have too much common sense.

Those with *uncommon* sense, among whom we might include the mystics, can seem much more concerned than these folks about the implications of a love of God for generosity to one's fellow beings. In *The Cloud of Unknowing*, for example, the English author pauses in his account of the techniques of contemplation to examine briefly "what charity is in itself; how it is subtly and perfectly contained in contemplative love." In chapter twenty-four he tells us: "Now just as contemplative love nurtures perfect humility, so it is *creative of practical goodness*, especially charity. For in real charity one loves God for himself alone above every created thing and he loves his fellow man because it is God's law" (80). Just as the skilled contemplative passes beyond particular human affections, so he/she regards everyone as a relation, part of the human community that it is our duty under God to foster.

In discussing St. John of the Cross's understanding of "dark night," Constance Fitzgerald is even more specific about the way the mystic's experience of God leads to an identification with others. When we experience the touch of God's hand "marking, wounding, challenging, shaping, purifying and transforming human personality," she writes, "this image subverts our whole individualistic perception of reality, that is, the way we experience not only other people, but also other species, the earth and even the cosmos." For Fitzgerald (reading John of the Cross) as for the English author of *The Cloud of Unknowing*, "It is at this point in development that the images of the poor, the oppressed, the exploited, the suffering, take on an overpowering clarity and significance. They are clearly a suffering extension of the inner image of Jesus-Sophia, and they make a claim" (101).

But what claim can they make upon those of us who are not skilled in reading suffering as a blessing and a summons? Simone Weil addresses this issue at some length in "Forms of the Implicit Love of God." Like Freud in *Civilization and Its Discontents*, Weil says that such a claim is against reason. The sympathy of the weak for the strong is a natural inclination because it confers upon the weak a type of power. However, sympathy that goes in the other direction is against nature and therefore if it is true sympathy it must be called "supernatural." But this is the only kind of sympathy, according to Weil, that is worthwhile. "Almsgiving," she insists, "when it is not supernatural is like a sort of purchase. It *buys* the sufferer" (147).

In the link between Jesus and Sophia, we encounter a form of wisdom that is nurturing while being, in a sense, impersonal. Though it is always true that much charity is practiced in a self-serving spirit, in the Bible Jesus tells us that when one gives to those in need, one should do so anonymously. Addressing the needs of those who are suffering, then, may not be a matter of virtue but of a larger truth. According to Weil, "The Gospel makes no distinction between the love of our neighbor [which we are told to undertake] and justice" (139). This is unreasonable, to some extent, since our neighbors do not always seem to us to be deserving. We judge them and by judging them we find excuses for refusing them our favors, as one sees constantly today in discussions about drug use and the homeless or about women who have babies while on welfare. But Weil's point seems to be that we have invented the distinction between justice and charity in order to escape from the requirement that we serve the needs of others by making such service our priority. "Only the absolute identification of justice and love makes the coexistence possible of compassion and gratitude on the one hand, and on the other, of respect for the dignity of affliction in the afflicted—a respect felt by the sufferer himself" (*Waiting for God*, hereafter *WFG*, 140).

THE DIGNITY OF AFFLICTION

Though, with the exception of William Carlos Williams, few of the modernist poets who influenced Elizabeth Bishop wrote much about the poor, she did, and not just once but many times. Obviously she felt connected in some deep way to people in straitened circumstances and not simply because of her years in Nova Scotia running barefoot in a homemade dress. Until she moved to Brazil, she lived on a small fixed income, and her problems with alcohol (another instance of living in a box) gave her a heightened sense of compassion for people living under duress. But her compassion, by and large, was not sentimental. Frederick Buechner helpfully reminds us that "when we sentimentalize about things, we see not so much the things themselves as we see the flood of feeling, of sentiment, that the things themselves occasion in us, with the result that sentimentality becomes a form of blocking out the world" (108). In Bishop's writing, the flood of feeling is held in check by various means, with the effect that the world comes into focus in her poetry and the poor stand their ground without apology.

"The dignity of affliction in the sufferer" is a somewhat different matter, however. It suggests that those who suffer have the opportunity *to move toward* experience (and, for Weil, also God) in a more serious way than those whose lives are less demanding. I find the work of Elizabeth Bishop compelling because it makes compassion not simply a matter of feeling but also of thought, what George Herbert calls "something understood." From one point of view, her work fosters the notion that we are in many ways divided one from another as we experience meaning as suffering. She was, after all, an outsider, and, according to Adrienne Rich, had an "outsider's eye." However, from another point of view (and this is a point of view that requires thought), we must keep in mind that for Bishop we are also "all just one," suffering, as we do suffer, in concert.

In a 1941 observation piece called "Mercedes Hospital," Bishop offers the reader two images of poverty and loneliness. The first is a brief obituary for one José Chacón, aged eighty-four, who died in Mercedes Hospital. His funeral service is announced in the newspaper, followed by this sentence: "The deceased leaves but one survivor, a nephew, [also named] José Chacón." The obituary appears in the Key West *Citizen* where it is followed by a sentimental poem entitled "Friend?" that tells the familiar story of someone who lost his fair-weather friends when he lost his wealth.

> You go home to your little room
> And sit silent in the gloom,
> Thinking of the once bright day,
> But now you are old and all alone.
>
> But one comes to you every day
> As on your bed you must lay.
> He stops and takes you by the hand,
> And the look on his face, you understand.
>
> That smile on his face tells a lot
> As he sits by your bed and watches the clock
> Ticking the hours softly by.
> With a tear in his eye, he says goodbye.
> That was a Friend to the End.

Bishop writes: "I find this brief account of the death of an old man in what is really just the poorhouse, the Casa del Pobre, very touching," adding ironically: "And of course the poem is touching too, but it naturally does not occur to me to connect them" (*CPr*, 62).

The story of Mercedes Hospital, in fact, sets up a series of contrasts between sentimental religious clichés (the "Friend to the End") and active, unsentimental forms of charity. The nephew of José Chacón, the man who died in the poorhouse, is a rich man who has washed his hands of his uncle because his uncle chose to "drink, drink, drink." In contrast there is Miss Mamie Harris, the duenna of Mercy Hospital, who takes in the sick and destitute, including a black man, though "they have a place. But he is so sick and we have so few patients." Miss Mamie doesn't seem to reflect much on her life or the lives of others (she is neither moralistic nor political), and she performs her duties without any sense that her activities are extraordinary.

For example, Miss Mamie's patient Antonica can't hear and can't see, and Miss Mamie treats her like a baby but not out of any special tenderness. "She's terrible fond of me," says Miss Mamie. Bishop adds: "The old woman's hair has been cut so that it is about an inch long. Miss Mamie keeps rubbing her hand over the small skull, rather roughly, I think" (68). What is one to make of Miss Mamie's lifetime of self-denial? The narrator, who is probably one version of Elizabeth Bishop, muses: "I know that some people consider her a saint. Probably they are right. She is capable of arousing the same feelings that the saints do: profoundest admiration and suspicion. Thirty dollars a month wages, thirty years of unselfish labor, 'managing' on one hundred and thirty dollars a month for [the hospital's entire budget] are all incredible feats—unless one does believe she is a saint" (*CPr*, 68–69).

At first, this narrator has her doubts and she hesitates to give money to Miss Mamie herself lest she pocket it instead of putting it in the Poor Box. Then she thinks again. "I realize my doubt is another proof of Miss Mamie's saintliness, and therefore of her ability to arouse suspicion. I have always thought that the reason we suspect saints is the ambiguous nature of all good deeds, the impossibility of knowing why they are being performed" (70). Miss Mamie isn't particularly gentle or full of feeling. "Among Miss Mamie's saintly qualities," Bishop notes, "tenderness is lacking. In fact, it is the absence of tenderness that is the consoling thing about her" (70). She doesn't demean her patients by making them feel her sense of sacrifice, her consciousness of compassion. She seems to have no ulterior motive, good or bad, for doing what she does, and this is why she is so effective. "Mamie hasn't any idea that what she is doing where she is needs explaining. She has managed to transfer the same feeling to her patients—giving them security from hopelessness" (71). And, one might add, freedom from shame.

Bishop's treatment of the poor people who occupy the hospital beds in the story is similarly unsentimental. Take, for example, the two brothers Sonny and Tommy. Mr. Tommy, who has been living in the hospital for fourteen years, sings hymns all day. "He keeps a large Bible and two hymnbooks beside him and is rather inclined to boast that he reads nothing else. He sings the hymns partly to spite Mr. Sonny, who is sitting in the next room just behind the folding doors and who, before he came to Mercedes Hospital, was not able to lead as sheltered and virtuous a life as Mr. Tommy has" (66). Mr. Sonny is dying of dropsy, a disease of excess.

As Bishop well knew, the poor and those in the grip of suffering are not necessarily appealing to contemplate. Yet, according to Simone Weil, such people have a distinction that makes a claim. "He who is

aching in every limb, worn out by the effort of a day of work, that is
to say a day when he has been subject to matter, bears the reality of the
universe in his flesh like a thorn. The difficulty for him is to look and
to love. If he succeeds, he loves the Real. That is the immense privi-
lege God has reserved for his poor. But they scarcely ever know it"
(170). Know it or not, those who are living with the resistance of the
universe as a constant companion are in a better situation than the rich
to understand the requirement of self-surrender. This is what Weil
calls "the dignity of the affliction in the afflicted," though of course
not everyone who suffers rises to its occasion.

Simone Weil herself went much farther than most of us are
prepared to go, choosing to work alongside the poorest of the poor
and, despite ill health and a delicate constitution, limiting her intake
of food to what these workers could afford. Her philosophy emphasizes treating the Other as an equal and doing so because this is what
God requires: "The supernatural virtue of justice consists of behaving
exactly as though there were equality when one is the stronger in an
unequal relationship" (143).

I-THOU

Most of us receive a call to practice unreasonable charity at some
point, whether it be in the realm of family, friendship, neighborliness,
local political action, or world service, but we do not know the hour
of its coming, and, in the confusion of the moment, we may find ourselves, like the hesitant disciples in Luke 9, unready to forsake our
own concerns. However, we must not forget that, despite what we are
often led to believe, a merely expedient generosity is not "what the
Lord requires." As Simone Weil understood so well, for our sense of
responsibility to be adequate to *that* standard, it must be, at times,
against reason, "unlikely," even grotesque.

To take a literary example, the narrator in Herman Melville's story
"Bartleby the Scrivener" is confronted unexpectedly by a demand for
supernatural charity, and, not surprisingly, he fails to meet the completely unreasonable demand of his subordinate (a demand almost
Biblical in its refusal of compromise). After Bartleby refuses to do any
more work and yet "prefer[s] not to" vacate his employer's premises,
most readers (who are reasonable people) think that the narrator
should take whatever steps are necessary to get rid of this obstinate
creature. Indeed, rather than agonizing about Bartleby, as the narrator
does, many readers get frustrated with the whole business and wish
Bartleby *and* his employer would go to the devil. But the story takes

a theological turn when Bartleby dies in the jail and the narrator tells the jailer that he is asleep "with kings and counselors," a phrase from the Book of Job. In the part of Job's story where these words appear, he is thinking longingly of death, for: "There the prisoners rest together; they hear not the voice of the oppressor," Job says (3:14,18). The extraordinary thing in Melville's story is that the smug, self-satisfied, middle-class narrator (perhaps symbolically "the oppressor") is himself brought to the edge of the abyss by what is eloquent though barely spoken in the forlorn Bartleby. He is so unsettled by this experience that all he can say at the end is "Ah Bartleby! Ah Humanity."

Writers who are attuned to the idea of charity as against "nature" and "reason" (when asked to be a little reasonable, Bartleby answers "I prefer *not* to be a little reasonable") can be as bleak as J. M. Coetzee in *Disgrace* or as funny as Flannery O'Connor in "Greenleaf." In O'Connor's story we have two women: Mrs. May and Mrs. Greenleaf. The former is from the middle class, and is respectable and godless. "She was a good Christian woman with a large respect for religion, though she did not, of course, believe any of it was true" (31). Mrs. Greenleaf, on the other hand, is from the lower class, and is earnest and grotesque. Every day she cuts out all the stories of misfortune from the newspaper and buries them in the woods: "then she fell on the ground over them and mumbled and groaned for an hour or so, moving her huge arms back and forth under her and out again and finally just lying down flat and, Mrs. May suspected, going to sleep in the dirt" (30). Of course, Mrs. Greenleaf, for all her peculiarities, is totally sincere about her efforts to heal the world and therefore is redeemed, whereas Mrs. May, who once remarked "tactfully" to Mr. Greenleaf, "I'm afraid your wife has let her religion warp her, . . . Everything in moderation, you know" (51), has a lot to learn about Christian charity but learns it all too late.

Like her friend Flannery O'Connor, Elizabeth Bishop took a lifelong interest in the poor, but she did so from a position not of Christian duty nor of liberal principle, but of the "unlikely" belief that we are all parts of a larger whole. When Bishop finally rewrote the story in "The Country Mouse" where she recalls going to the dentist with her aunt and feeling totally disoriented, the resulting poem—"In the Waiting Room"—shifts the emphasis in relating the experience from one of radical alienation ("How strange you are, inside looking out. You are not Beppo, or the chestnut tree, or Emma, you are *you* and you are going to be *you* forever") to one of radical connectedness ("You are one of *them*").

In "the waiting room," the *National Geographic* no longer appears simply as a magazine where human and animal "others" are on display. Here it provides a theater of haunting images into which the child is drawn not simply as a spectator but also as an actor.

> My aunt was inside
> what seemed like a long time
> and while I waited I read
> the *National Geographic*
> (I could read) and carefully
> studied the photographs:
> the inside of a volcano,
> black, and full of ashes;
> then it was spilling over
> in rivulets of fire.
> Osa and Martin Johnson
> dressed in riding breeches,
> laced boots, and pith helmets.
> A dead man slung on a pole
> —"Long Pig," the caption said.
> Babies with pointed heads
> wound round and round with string;
> black, naked women with necks
> wound round and round with wire
> like the necks of light bulbs.
> Their breasts were horrifying.
> I read it right straight through.
> I was too shy to stop. (*CP*, 159)

At first the images seem to be again about difference and alienation: the disorder of nature (the volcano), the inequalities of class (the Johnsons as white colonizers), humans portrayed as animals (as in "Long Pig" or, more mutedly, its associated racist rhetoric), the horrors of nature as it is "wound round and round" into cultural forms.

However, something completely different happens in the next section of the poem, an event that doesn't appear in the earlier story. The child hears her aunt, here renamed "Consuelo" (consolation), utter a cry of pain: "I wasn't at all surprised; / even then I knew she was / a foolish, timid woman" (*CP*, 160). What *is* surprising is that it turns out that the cry is actually not her aunt's but her own: "it was *me*: / my voice, in my mouth. / Without thinking at all / I was my foolish aunt." This ushers in a set of reflections about the fundamental links that connect us all, one to another.

Why should I be my aunt
or me, or anyone?
What similarities—
boots, hands, the family voice
I felt in my throat, or even
the *National Geographic*
and those awful hanging breasts—
held us all together
or made us all just one?
How—I didn't know any
word for it—how "unlikely" . . . (*CP*, 161)

How unlikely, indeed. In the context of the First World War (the time
is February 1918), these cannot be idle reflections. In fact, the dizzi-
ness that they provoke in the child at the end draws our attention to
the sense of "supernatural" disruption that such a view is liable
to produce. Its consolation, if consoling it is, comes from knowing
that, despite the evidence of war, despite everything, we are in this
predicament together, those "awful hanging breasts" reminding us of
our common humanity and the dark knowledge of God that we are
sometimes forced to take in, "derived from the rocky breasts /
forever," as in "At the Fishhouses."

If one takes seriously the notion that we are all connected one to
another, it is hard to justify the suffering associated with the differences
we ourselves make between the races, classes, and genders that are also
evoked by the poem. This perspective is not far from Weil's belief
that loving one's neighbor is no different than doing justice, loving
kindness, and walking humbly with one's God.

In his conception of the I-Thou relationship, the twentieth-century
Jewish theologian Martin Buber (whom we know Bishop read)
claimed that whether one believes in God or not, the recognition of
another's legitimacy as a being comparable to oneself is tantamount to
a recognition of God. "But when he, too, who abhors the name, and
believes himself to be godless, gives his whole being to addressing the
Thou of his life as a Thou that cannot [in an absolute sense] be limited
by another, he [or she] addresses God" (quoted in Wyschogrod, 411).

CRITICAL PRACTICES

When Bishop writes, as she usually does, about the *paradoxes* of the
claim poverty makes, she often creates a limited consciousness (what
is sometimes misleadingly called an "unreliable narrator") who comes

to see herself either through the Other's eyes or through her own eyes newly opened to the dignity of affliction in the other. In "Mercedes Hospital," for example, the initial suspicions of the narrator in her encounter with the "saint," Mamie Harris, lead to a change in perspective as she comes to understand what is "consoling" in Mamie's treatment of her patients: her absence of pity for them and for herself. In the poem "In the Waiting Room," the child finds her initial sense of alienation (from Africans, from her aunt, from those around her) dissolving paradoxically into a recognition of the unlikely (unreasonable) truth that there is something that holds us all together and makes us all "just one."

It could be argued that such a reconceptualization of "difference" must be at some level metaphysical. Even our shared biology is not universalizing enough to make us "all just one," since our biological similarity, one to another, is not an identity. From some points of view, biological differences (for example, sex, skin color, disability) irreparably divide us. And, though the prospect of death is universal, this fact may make us *equal* without furnishing us with any genuine sense of connection to one another.

One must think outside the box to acknowledge that we are implicated in the suffering of others, but this is a position that Bishop not infrequently assumes. By so doing, her morality, at least for a reader like me, begins to take on a theological resonance. Sometimes, as in "Mercedes Hospital," she actually uses theological language (the language of sainthood) to address this notion. At other times, as in her late poem "Going to the Bakery," the moon's eye stands in, in some sense, for God's eye.

Under the gaze of the Other—whether the Other be someone such as Mamie Harris, "when she takes hold of my shoulders and peers into my face and asks question after question" (*CPr*, 69), or whether the Other be some transcendental force—one is placed in the position of asking: Should I be doing what I am doing or not? A change of viewpoint implies a change of behavior, and often—in Bishop's work as in Flannery O'Connor's—the change is ushered in by an irruption of the grotesque. In the light of the moon, even going to the bakery becomes a reminder of the suffering of the poor and sick: "the round cakes look about to faint— / each turns up a glazed white eye. / The gooey tarts are red and sore. / Buy, buy, what shall I buy?" (*CP*, 151). This narrator is poised to see that, because of her health and her money, she is in a position to respond more than mechanically to others, to register their claims, and to give something of herself to address them, as she herself acknowledges in the end.

In front of my apartment house
a black man sits in a black shade,
lifting his shirt to show a bandage
on his black, invisible side.

Fumes of *cachaça* knock me over,
like gas fumes from an auto-crash.
He speaks in perfect gibberish.
The bandage glares up, white and fresh.

I give him seven cents in *my*
terrific money, say "Good night"
from force of habit. Oh, mean habit!
Not one word more apt or bright? (*CP*, 152)

She doesn't romanticize this man (he speaks in gibberish and drinks cachaça, a strongly alcoholic liquor), but she sees that his imperfections do not excuse her failure to be more responsive, a failure almost guaranteed (for most of us) by habit.

Though Bishop here spells things out in a straightforward manner, her usual form of self-reflection involves us as readers in the process of thinking about why the world is the way it is and how it might be changed. In a Key West poem, "Faustina, or Rock Roses," the narrator pays a visit to an old white woman who is tended by a black servant named Faustina. Again, we can see that Faustina is no saint. She whines about herself, begs for cognac, and even for a moment seems to be contemplating killing her mistress:

Complaining of, explaining
the terms of her employment.
She bends above the other.
Her sinister kind face
presents a cruel black
coincident conundrum.
    Oh, is it

freedom at last, a lifelong
dream of time and silence,
dream of protection and rest?
Or is it the very worst,
the unimaginable nightmare
that never before dared last
    more than a second?

The acuteness of the question
forks instantly and starts
a snake-tongued flickering;

blurs further, blunts, softens,
separates, falls, our problems
becoming helplessly
   proliferative.
There is no way of telling.
The eyes say only either.
At last the visitor rises,
awkwardly proffers her bunch
of rust-perforated roses
and wonders oh, whence come
   all the petals. (*CP*, 74)

The final question hovers in the air, as though it were a question for God to answer. Even the language of it—"whence come"—is a bit archaic, but when one asks about the origin of differences (here "petals"), one is already in the realm of separation and the fall, of suffering meaning. The difficulties of knowing what to do about economic inequality and injustice seem to be endless. Temptation in the form of the serpent grips Faustina (or the visitor's imagined "Faustina") for a moment, but the visitor, who can offer only "rust-perforated roses," comes to see herself as also part of the problem as one thing leads to another: "*our* problems / becoming helplessly / proliferative."

Certainly Bishop herself was not a "saint," but she did more than simply think about the problems of the poor. In Key West she befriended an impoverished "primitive" painter from Cuba by the name of Gregorio Valdes. She gave him a commission and actually helped him get a place in a show of "Unknown Painters" at the Museum of Modern Art. In her memoir for Gregorio, published in *Partisan Review* in 1939, Bishop recalls: "I had been afraid that when I brought him the clipping from the *Times* he had been too sick to understand it, but the youngest daughter told me that he had looked at it a great deal and had kept telling them all that he was 'going to get the first prize for painting in New York'" (*CPr*, 56). Hilary Bradt remembers Bishop as a person of unusually humanitarian sensibilities who would "cry at the plight of the poor" (Fountain and Brazeau, 251). But she did more than cry. She treated the poor with great personal respect and she wrote about them with gusto. "Jerónimo's House," for example, demonstrates the attention she paid to the houses of the poor and her admiration for their resilience against what she calls "the hurricane," the powerful forces arrayed against them.

Many people look to politics to find ways of addressing social injustice, and certainly political action has been an important means of easing some of the suffering of the poor, but, surrounded by political discussion in Brazil, Bishop grew tired of the endless haggling. Some of Bishop's poems do address political issues such as colonialism, and in her prose pieces about the building of Brasília (where poor people were herded into substandard housing to serve the rich) one can see the direction her critiques of the government were apt to take. But generally Bishop is pessimistic about the role that politics alone, even that of the Left, can play in the lives of the poor. The ground can shift so easily in political struggles, especially in Brazil where Bishop watched a man she thought would bring needed reforms, Carlos Lacerda, turn, instead, into a dictator.

A good example of a poem that implicitly contrasts religious and political approaches is "Squatter's Children." It addresses the lives of the people who live in the *favelas*, the makeshift cardboard communities that house thousands of Brazilian poor people on the hills surrounding Rio de Janeiro. In "Squatter's Children," we are once again confronted by the *deus absconditus*, the absent God who looks down on the children of the poor seemingly without much interest: "The sun's suspended eye / blinks casually." But here too there is a storm brewing. There are questions going unanswered, and when the cardboard structure that houses this family is described as a "little, soluble, / unwarrantable ark," one is inclined to think of the Flood and its causes. In what context, the poem seems to ask, is this ark "unwarrantable"?

The narrator turns to address the children at the end of the poem and, though the main thrust of this final stanza is an indictment of current economic conditions, something else—more muted but more positive—seems to be suggested at the same time.

> Children, the threshold of the storm
> has slid beneath your muddy shoes;
> wet and beguiled, you stand among
> the mansions you may choose
> out of a bigger house than yours,
> whose lawfulness endures.
> Its soggy documents retain
> your rights in rooms of falling rain. (*CP*, 95)

Bishop is clearly playing with Biblical language here: "In my Father's house are many mansions" (John 14:2) and the Psalms where in several places the Lord is described as "enduring" forever. Bishop's poem calls the children of the poor "beguiled," deceived. Is it religion that has deceived them, or politics, or both? They stand among the cardboard houses dissolving in the rain. These are the only mansions they may choose out of a bigger house than theirs "whose lawfulness endures." As I read these lines, they at first appear to present the State as that "bigger house" because it is the institution guaranteed by law. The voice of the narrator, then, emerges as bitterly ironic. These squatters, the very poorest of the poor, have no rights worth speaking of, and such "documents" as are furnished to them by the State seem on the verge of dissolution.

However, one pauses at the word "retain." Coming at the end of the line, it carries a stronger emphasis than it might elsewhere. Is there some place where the rights of the poor, the claims they can make upon the rich, are indeed preserved? If so, it is more likely to be in the realm of God whose lawfulness endures in a very different sense, though this possibility hovers as a barely distinct presence in what is otherwise a rather pessimistic poem.

Bishop wrote another poem about the *favelas*, a ballad called "The Burglar of Babylon," that actually became a Brazilian favorite and was set to music. It begins:

> On the fair green hills of Rio
> There grows a fearful stain:
> The poor who come to Rio
> And can't go home again.
>
> On the hills a million people,
> A million sparrows, nest,
> Like a confused migration
> That's had to light and rest,
>
> Building its nests, or houses,
> Out of nothing at all, or air.
> You'd think a breath would end them,
> They perch so lightly there.
>
> But they cling and spread like lichen,
> And the people come and come.
> There's one hill called the Chicken,
> And one called Catacomb;
>
> There's the hill of Kerosene,
> And the hill of the Skeleton,
> The hill of Astonishment,
> And the hill of Babylon. (*CP*, 112)

Like "The Ballad of Gregorio Cortez," passed down in South Texas from one generation of poor Latinos to the next, this ballad features

a man on the run whose life reflects the brutal conditions of poverty
and the negative consequences of power politics.

"The Burglar of Babylon" tells the (true) story of the outlaw
Micuçu, who escapes from the penitentiary and returns to his roots
among the *favelas*, only to be pursued by the police and eventually
shot down. Bishop doesn't romanticize him—even his auntie who
raised him says he was "always mean"—but in the process of telling
his story, she adopts the view of the poor people themselves, a view
that is sometimes humorous, but also sympathetic. The aunt grieves
for her nephew while at the same time she holds him to account.

> "We have always been respected.
>   His sister has a job.
> Both of us gave him money.
>   Why did he have to rob?
>
> "I raised him to be honest,
>   Even here, in Babylon slum."
> The customers had another [drink],
>   Looking serious and glum.
>
> But one of them said to another,
>   When he got outside the door,
> "He wasn't much of a burglar,
>   He got caught six times—or more."

The poem contrasts the security of the rich (like Bishop herself), who
watch the events through binoculars (as she actually did), with the
vulnerability of the poor, whose homes are open to the winds and
whose lives are under surveillance. Politics and religion also exist in
separate realms, it seems, as we can see by the example of an officer
inadvertently shot by one of his men.

> The dying man said, "Finish
>   The job we came here for."
> He committed his soul to God
>   And his sons to the Governor. (*CP*, 115)

Time and eternity do not mix here, but maybe they should to
a greater extent than they do. One ponders, for instance, the significance of the title of the poem, "The Burglar of Babylon." In addition
to its literal accuracy as a hill in the favelas, is Bishop suggesting that
poverty is a form of captivity like the Babylonian captivity recounted
in the Bible? "By the rivers of Babylon, there we sat down, yea, we

wept, when we remembered Zion" (Psalms 137:1). If Bishop *is* drawing our attention to the Babylonian Captivity, to whom or to what does one look for liberation? Market capitalism has certainly failed the poor in South America, many of whom are worse off, because of economic restructuring, than they were during Bishop's time forty years ago. Some people are looking to the Catholic Church for a new vision of a society both prosperous and just, but it is hard to say whether Liberation Theology stands a better chance than the usual political maneuvering of improving the lives of the very poor.

THE STILL, SMALL VOICE

Even in the midst of the busy lives so many of us lead here in the United States, there are opportunities for genuine charity. I think, for example, of my colleague, a professor of history, who works tire-lessly for the impoverished people of Chiapas, Mexico, and who lives very simply in order to support a family in Guatemala (not her own). Many people, it seems, even the young, are doing unlikely or "irrational" things in the name of Love.

I also think of my mother in this context, though she would hardly have described herself as irrational. A conservative woman who did not believe in welfare, she never faltered in her sense of her obliga-tions, giving up much that she enjoyed in life (college, travel, late night carousing) first in order to support her parents, and again later, when my father got sick, in order to support us all. Thinking of my own life, it is daunting to confront the fact that, year after year, my parents never gave a dinner party, never went out together at night, allowed themselves few pleasures beyond an Old Fashioned cocktail at Thanksgiving and Christmas and a short vacation with the children (often paid for by some relative) in the summertime.

Moving from apartment to apartment, my mother juggled the bills in an era before credit cards, paying this creditor one month and that one the next, until every one got paid. She had no friends who lived close by and her home life was far from idyllic. Yet she persisted, and in the end both of her children went through college and graduate school, became self-supporting, and lived on into middle age without her.

My mother had once attended church but she grew disillusioned with religion, and in her old age took a "scientific" view of things, scoffing at people who ignored the evidence of physical anthropology. Her charity was entirely personal, the product of an old-fashioned upbringing, and the list of those she thought "beneath" us was long, though what this could mean I could never quite fathom. In spite of herself, she responded to *individuals* (it was groups of people she disdained) and would often say to me things like "Well, he's Jewish but, you know, he's a lot of fun," or "Are you sure that woman is a homosexual? She seems quite intelligent and down-to-earth to me." As forewoman of a jury, she persuaded her fellow jurors to award damages to a poor black man who had been hit by a bus, only to be told by the judge that their decision did not, in fact, accord with the law because the bus company was not liable. My mother was tenderhearted, inconsistent, and, like Marianne Moore, always voted Republican.

It is probably because of my mother that I like Bishop's controversial poem "Manuelzinho" for its portrayal of someone caught between her class prejudices and her charitable instincts. Though Bishop's politics in this poem have been faulted for not challenging the class system itself, in my view, "Manuelzinho" shows that even an aristocrat, bred to look down on the poor, can experience what we might call a spiritual transformation. If her voice, with its edge of irritation and air of superiority, is not always pleasant to listen to, perhaps that's the point. In her own way, she's like my mother, a very human character.

Bishop departs from her usual practice and actually provides a bit of stage direction at the beginning of the poem. Between brackets she writes: "Brazil. A friend of the writer is speaking." Lota is an obvious choice here, but in actuality the speaker is probably a combination of Lota and Elizabeth herself.

The poem begins with a kind of description of Manuelzinho, the gardener.

> Half squatter, half tenant (no rent)—
> a sort of inheritance; white,
> in your thirties now, and supposed
> to supply me with vegetables,
> but you don't; or you won't; or you can't
> get the idea through your brain—
> the world's worst gardener since Cain. (*CP*, 96)

Now it is true that in the Bible Cain is a tiller of the fields, but that hardly seems reason enough to drag him in here unless Bishop is asking us to think more broadly about "the fall" as a rift between brothers or in the human community in general, a rift here represented by class divisions.

There are, in fact, lots of little nudges in the direction of such thoughts in the poem. Three objects appear at the feet of the narrator: Manuelzinho's clogs and his "holey hat" making a triangle (or trinity) of representations of the poor. (Manuel, of course, is a form of Emmanuel. Not that he is meant to be a Christ figure, but his name does remind us that Jesus said: "Even as ye have done it unto the least of these, ye have done it unto me.") Manuelzinho's father dies—"a superior man / with a black plush hat, and a moustache / like a white spread-eagled sea gull"—but little Manuel, for some reason, does not believe he is dead. The narrator thinks this is absurd.

> I give you money for the funeral
> and you go and hire a *bus*
> for the delighted mourners,
> so I have to hand over some more
> and then have to hear you tell me
> you pray for me every night! (*CP*, 97)

The speaker is perfectly convincing within her limits, and when she thinks of him coming, hat in hand, with a face "like a child's fistful / of bluets or white violets, / improvident as the dawn," *she* certainly is not thinking of the passage in Matthew where Jesus says: "And why take ye thought for raiment? Consider the lilies of the field, how they grow; they toil not, neither do they spin: And yet I say unto you, That even Solomon in all his glory was not arrayed like one of these" (Matt. 6:28–29).

There is, however, one place where the speaker directly refers to the Bible. Manuelzinho enters "briskly" to settle up

> what we call our "accounts,"
> with two old copybooks,
> one with flowers on the cover,
> the other with a camel.
> Immediate confusion.
> You've left out the decimal points.
> Your columns stagger,
> honeycombed with zeroes.
> You whisper conspiratorilly;
> the numbers mount to millions.
> Account books? They are Dream Books.
> In the kitchen we dream together
> how the meek shall inherit the earth—
> or several acres of mine. (*CP*, 98)

It's all done very subtly, and amusingly, so that we don't really think that this narrator is a candidate for spiritual transformation when she recalls: "You paint—heaven knows why— / the outside of the crown / and brim of your straw hat" (*CP*, 99). But something seems to be working in her without her knowledge. Heaven knows why.

> One [hat] was gold for a while,
> but the gold wore off, like plate.
> One was bright green. Unkindly
> I called you Klorophyll Kid.
> My visitors thought it was funny.
> I apologize here and now.
>
> You helpless, foolish man,
> I love you all I can,
> I think. Or do I?
> I take off my hat, unpainted
> and figurative, to you.
> Again I promise to try. (*CP*, 99)

In its own way, this declaration represents a real attempt on the speaker's part to love her neighbor. Again, this is a narrator who comes to rethink her prejudices. The poem walks a thin line between applauding and deriding both Manuelzinho *and* its narrator, but it stays upright, partly because of its wit.

WIT'S WISDOM

In a long letter to Anne Stevenson dated January 8, 1964, Bishop admitted that for her humor was of the essence.

> The aunt I liked best was a very funny woman: most of my close friends have been funny people; Lota de Macedo Soares is funny. Pauline Hemingway (the second Mrs. H) a good friend until her death in 1951 was the wittiest person, man or woman, I've ever known. Marianne was very funny—Cummings, too, of course. Perhaps I need such people to cheer me up. They are usually stoical, unsentimental, and physically courageous.

And then she goes on to relate these remarks to the poor.

> The *poor* Brazilians', the people's, sense of humor is really all that keeps this country bearable a lot of the time. They're not "courageous," however—far from it—but the constant political jokes, the words to the .

sambas, the nicknames etc. are brilliant and a consolation—unfortunately mostly untranslatable. Only their humor sometimes manages to sweeten this repugnant mess of greed & corruption. (Unpublished letter, Washington University Archive)

"Pink Dog" is another witty poem, whose wit is funny at times until its barbs sink in. It tells a true story of life in Brazil where the poor are done away with because they don't "look well" in a country that is always trying to present itself as sophisticated, prosperous, and a good bet for foreign capital. Bishop uses the device of a hairless dog who horrifies the passersby as she trots, "naked and pink," across the avenue.

> Of course they're mortally afraid of rabies.
> You are not mad; you have a case of scabies
> but look intelligent. Where are your babies?
>
> (A nursing mother, by those hanging teats.)
> In what slum have you hidden them, poor bitch,
> while you go begging, living by your wits?
> Didn't you know? It's been in all the papers,
> to solve this problem, how they deal with beggars?
> They take and throw them in the tidal rivers.
>
> Yes, idiots, paralytics, parasites
> go bobbing in the ebbing sewage, nights
> out in the suburbs, where there are no lights.
>
> If they do this to anyone who begs,
> Drugged, drunk, or sober, with or without legs,
> what would they do to sick four-leggèd dogs?
>
> In the cafés and on the sidewalk corners
> the joke is going around that all the beggars
> who can afford them now wear life preservers. (*CP*, 190)

At the 1999 international Elizabeth Bishop Conference in Brazil, one enterprising scholar had ferreted out a newspaper article of Bishop's era in which the story of the floating bodies was presented in simple, factual detail. No joke.

People still argue about whether the recommendation the speaker gives to the dog to "dance at Carnival" is to any degree serious. Some say that the Brazilian attitude of the poor themselves, especially with regard to the "samba schools," is similarly unsentimental. It's a *good* thing, they say, for the poor to defy their poverty by dressing up and dancing at Carnival. And we know Bishop admired those who were "stoical, unsentimental, and physically courageous."

But the poem's fantastic, over-the-top rhymes seem to me an indictment; not of the poor, of course, but of the forces they have to confront to survive.

> Now look, the practical, the sensible
> solution is to wear a *fantasía*
> Tonight you simply can't afford to be a-
> n eyesore. But no one will ever see a
> dog in *máscara* this time of year.
> Ash Wednesday'll come but Carnival is here.
> What sambas can you dance? What will you wear? (*CP*, 190–91)

Carnival, the great equalizer of the people, is a time when, as Mikhail Bakhtin has noted, the world is turned upside down. God appears in the figure of the clown or the fool. The idea that Ash Wednesday will come, though it is tucked away here at the beginning of the line, also links the poor (and women who, worldwide, make up the majority of the poorest of the poor) to a different order of things. That Ash Wednesday will come may mean only that things will get tough again (the beginning of Lent implies a farewell to the flesh and a tightening of the belt). But Ash Wednesday in Christianity is also a time of communal self-examination, a call to change direction.

Even if the last line "Dress up! Dress up and dance at Carnival!" suggests a stinging indictment of what is all too often "dressed up" to hide the sufferings of the poor, Bishop does it with a light hand. Perhaps, like Christ, she resorted to parables to avoid what she thought of as the preachiness of Christians. He who has ears to hear, let him hear. But, as Camille Roman has shown in *Elizabeth Bishop's World War II—Cold War View*, Bishop had strong ethical concerns. If they sometimes put her at odds with formal religious structures, they mostly kept her work in line with biblical views of justice and charity.

6

ASSENT

JACOB'S LADDER

Begun in Mexico and finished in Key West, Bishop's "Anaphora," a strange, atmospheric lyric much admired by Marianne Moore, has puzzled many by seeming to allude to something that readers find hard to pin down. Who is the "ineffable creature," for example, mentioned in the first stanza, and what is the process of illumination that the beggar in the park experiences? Is this a poem about poetry, about poverty, about enlightenment? What do you think?

> Each day with so much ceremony
> begins, with birds, with bells,
> with whistles from a factory;
> such white-gold skies our eyes
> first open on, such brilliant walls
> that for a moment we wonder
> "Where is the music coming from, the energy?
> The day was meant for what ineffable creature
> we must have missed?" Oh promptly he
> appears and takes his earthly nature
>   instantly, instantly falls
>   victim of long intrigue,
>   assuming memory and mortal
>   mortal fatigue.
>
> More slowly falling into sight
> and showering into stippled faces,
> darkening, condensing all his light;
> in spite of all the dreaming
> squandered upon him with that look,
> suffers our uses and abuses,
> sinks through the drift of bodies,
> sinks through the drift of classes

> to evening to the beggar in the park
> who, weary, without lamp or book
> prepares stupendous studies
> the fiery event
> of every day in endless
> endless assent. (*CP*, 52)

Given what we have just been thinking about in the previous chapter, one thing seems clear. The beggar in the park is another of Bishop's resilient poor, and though "stupendous studies" might seem a bit high toned for this poor beggar, his ability to offer "endless / endless assent" qualifies him, from a certain point of view, for association with "the Most High."

Yet as far as most readers are concerned, a great deal, including the title, is obscure. What is "anaphora," for example? If you look up this word in the *Oxford English Dictionary*, a resource much used by Elizabeth Bishop, it will tell you that in the Christian liturgy, the anaphora is the prayer delivered for the Communion offering. As a literary device, anaphora is the repetition of a word or phrase, often at the beginning of successive lines, for emphasis or special effect. In this poem "sinks through the drift of bodies, / sinks through the drift of classes" is one example. Secondarily we might focus on "instantly, instantly," "mortal / mortal" and "endless / endless," repetitions of a single word that give these moments in the poem the special resonance of time and eternity.

When one looks up the word "anaphora" in guides to literary terms, one often finds that sections of the Bible, such as the Psalms, are quoted as examples. Examples abound from the New Testament as well. Paul's letter to the Hebrews, chapter eleven, is a rich resource because of its repetition of the words "by faith": by faith Abel offered to God, by faith Enoch was taken up, by faith Noah took heed, by faith Abraham, by faith Moses, etc. The introductory section of Hebrews 11 also seems relevant to Bishop's poem because it talks about the relationship of "things seen" to "things unseen": "Now faith is the assurance of things hoped for, the conviction of things not seen. For by it the men of old received divine approval. By faith we understand that the world was created by the word of God, so that what is seen was made out of things which do not appear."

In Bishop's poem, as in Hebrews 11, history is also a chronicle of the fall from faith into empiricism, from concern with things unseen (where is the energy coming from?) to a reductivist emphasis on the seen (slowly falling into sight). But there is more than a fall in this poem because the beggar, like Christ in the New Testament, *has* faith and brings us at the end to an ascent as well as an assent.

Getting there is tricky, however. Each of these two long stanzas ends with a sudden realignment where the last four lines move into a different register and suggest a change of course. In these sections even the tone changes. We begin with celebratory delight—birds, bells, whistles, white gold skies—but, reading the poem, we find ourselves passing from gaiety ("Oh promptly he / appears and takes his earthly nature") into something quite different:

> instantly, instantly falls
> victim of long intrigue,
> assuming memory and mortal
> mortal fatigue.

Taking up the idea of the anaphora as one part of the Communion liturgy, I find it difficult to read these lines without thinking of the crucifixion, in which Christ, victim of long intrigue, passes from present into past, assuming his own burden of memory and at the same time becoming a memory for others by passing through that agonizing experience of mortal / mortal fatigue ("let this cup pass from me"), which is itself a kind of fall into distrust. "My God, my God, why hast thou forsaken me?" Another muted allusion might be to the Apostles Creed where Jesus passes, instantly it seems, from birth to death, for He is the one "who for us men [i.e. humans] came down from heaven, was born of the Virgin Mary, was made man," and then immediately "was crucified also for us under Pontius Pilate."

The idea that Christ might be "the ineffable creature / we must have missed" is reminiscent of "Over 2,000 Illustrations" where the speaker wishes like Thomas for the certainty of sight: "Why couldn't we have seen / this old Nativity while we were at it?" But instead, born into modernity, we missed it.

Surely the anaphora of "mortal / mortal fatigue" is Bishop's weariness as well. It introduces the second stanza where we take up, I believe, Christ's residual presence in the contemporary period. One might note that the subject (he) seems to disappear, dispersed into others. This is not the instant fall of body into myth but the slower fall of myth into body, or more precisely into suffering sight. The sense of these lines is harder to get at but I take them to mean that the faces of those who are suffering, faces "stippled" or dotted with tears, may be seen as "darkening, condensing all [H] is light." That look of longing is arguably Bishop's own look at evening, the farthest thing possible from the openness and wonder of the morning vision with which the poem began. What do these people (faces) want? They want God to DO something for them, to change their lives. They are dreaming not of Him but of themselves and their own desires, what in French is called "le sentiment de soi," the sentiment of self.

But in a symmetrical reversal of the first stanza, the poem actually provides an example of a faithful one, the strong poet if you will, who leads us out of the cul-de-sac of self, and he of course is the beggar. God "suffers our uses and abuses" of His image and, in a second incarnation, sinks like a distillate through the drift of bodies and classes to those at the very bottom of the social ladder, those addressed in the "blessed are"s of the Beatitudes, itself a preeminent example of anaphora. For, though weary and without the accoutrements of the Church ("without lamp or book"), the beggar

> prepares stupendous studies
> the fiery event
> of every day in endless
> endless assent.

What is meant by *assent*, one might ask, and why is it so important? The key issue here, as elsewhere, has to do with self-surrender as when, after asking that the cup of bitterness be taken away, Christ says: "nevertheless not what I will, but what thou wilt" (Mark 14:36). It is not quite Simone Weil's self-denial that Bishop is after, then, but a kind of determination to practice acceptance, thus in a sense forfeiting the (always anyway baffled) attempt to control time.

In Bishop's life, assent was what struggled with the desire for death, a desire intensified by suffering and countermanded (at times) by the experience of beauty that satisfies, if only momentarily, the hunger of the soul. Thomas Travisano says that "for Bishop, beauty and spirituality do not exist apart from everyday experience, but are woven into its very fabric. To reveal them is not an imposition but a discovery" (90). This discovery, that beauty and spirit inhere in the present, no matter how constrained, is what feeds assent.

Some critics have argued that the ending of "Anaphora" is ironic, just as critics tend to do with "Filling Station," but, though "stupendous" is perhaps hyperbolic, it expresses to me something warmer and gentler than derision. The beggar is not foolish, though he may well be, like Shakespeare's fools, a bit peculiar.

Perhaps it is useful to look here at a companion poem by William Carlos Williams—a poem Bishop liked, written three years after hers and, I suspect, influenced by it—to see that it doesn't really matter whether one speaks of "ascent" or "descent" as long as both are figures of acceptance. Williams's poem, "The Descent," is more philosophical, and more about love than about the poor, but it too has a metaphysical edge. Here are Williams's lines, set up like stairs down the page:

The descent beckons
    as the ascent beckoned.
        Memory is a kind
of accomplishment,
        a sort of renewal
            even
an invitation, since the spaces it opens are new places
        inhabited by hordes
            heretofore unrealized,
of new kinds—
        since their movements
            are toward new objectives
(even though formerly they were abandoned).

No defeat is made up entirely of defeat—since
the world it opens is always a place
        formerly
            unsuspected. A
world lost,
        a world unsuspected,
            beckons to new places
and no whiteness (lost) is so white as the memory
of whiteness.

With evening, love wakens
        though its shadows
            which are alive by reason
of the sun shining—
        grow sleepy now and drop away
            from desire.
Love without shadows stirs now
        beginning to awaken
            as night
advances.

The descent
        made up of despairs
            and without accomplishment
realizes a new awakening:
        which is a reversal
of despair.

> For what we cannot accomplish, what
> is denied to love,
> what we have lost in the anticipation—
> a descent follows,
> endless and indestructible   (73–74)

There are clear connections between "The Descent"—which, according to Dana Gioia, Bishop taught in at least one of her classes—and "Anaphora," published earlier. Both focus on compensation, reversals of Fortune in which losses (or falls) become gains of a different kind (assents or ascents). Both look at evening moments when the glory of a sunlit world is replaced by something newly awakened that, even though it is born of weariness, is itself inexhaustible. And therefore blessed. The Williams poem is a much more serious poem than "Anaphora," but "One Art," which Bishop wrote at the end of her life and which contains some of the same sentiments, is of comparable weight.

Even here "the art of losing" is something at which the beggar is adept. His stupendous studies are called a "fiery event," and one pictures him in the park looking upward, either at a brilliant sunset or at the blazing stars above him. His acceptance (and gratitude) is the opposite of the poor armadillo's response in Bishop's poem "The Armadillo," who waddles angrily away from the scene of a fire, raising "a weak mailed fist / clenched ignorant against the sky!" (*CP*, 104). The fiery event that concludes the beggar's day, his "every day," is not unlike the new spaces that descent opens in the Williams poem, "inhabited by hordes," a concentration of vision that reveals a swarm.

Just as I was thinking about these matters, I received a letter from "Pam," a former student who, after graduation from college, joined a convent in the Arizona desert and became a Cistercian nun. She has been there now for many years and writes to me occasionally. In this letter she talks about the death of her prioress, Mother Beverly, in terms that are perhaps another version of what Bishop and Williams are talking about and so I include part of it here.

> . . . I did learn a great deal from [Beverly]. What I treasure most is her great trust in God. It was really quite amazing to see her trusting the Lord day by day, moment by moment, right through her last breath . . . and beyond. Not trusting God to fix everything & give her a "nice life" (you may have noticed, I'm sure, that God doesn't do that!) but trusting God in the real present moment, whatever it contained. That kind of trust has become the key of life for me. I spent

so many years fighting life, not willing to accept it as it was. "It's not supposed to be like this!" was one of my favorite lines; as was "Why does life have to be so damn difficult?!" . . . . What I've gradually come to instead is a faith vision that trusts in God's loving presence *with me in my here and now*, be it frustrating, difficult, satisfying, joyful, mundane, . . . etc. (Letter used by permission)

Pam's journey toward assent is reminiscent of the beggar's (or Williams's descent). In many traditions (one thinks especially of Buddhism), it is called enlightenment.

NOTHING BUT PLENTY

It is not surprising that Marianne Moore understood and admired "Anaphora" when others did not, because, of all Elizabeth Bishop's friends, she was the one most able to see the undercurrent of religious musing in Bishop's professed skepticism, just as she saw the value of lack in an economy of surfeit. In "The Jerboa" Moore contrasts the "too much" of Roman/Egyptian decadence with the realm of the jerboa, "a small desert rat, / and not famous, that / lives without water" and "has happiness." In contrast to the splendid domains of those who "understood / making colossi and / how to use slaves," the jerboa (perhaps a figure for the desert mystics) has a shining silver house

> of sand. O rest and
> joy, the boundless sand,
> the stupendous sand-spout,
> no water, no palm-trees, no ivory bed,
> tiny cactus; but one would not be he
> who has nothing but plenty. (*CP*, 13)

"The Jerboa"—with its "*stupendous* sand-spout"—predates "Anaphora" (and its "stupendous studies") by several years and, since Bishop had once carefully copied it out in longhand, she may well have had it in the back of her mind. Clearly, both women saw a certain kind of heroism in humble lives governed by assent and shared that essentially spiritual vision of experience with one another. After all, one would not be "he" who has nothing but plenty, because like cholesterol "too much" narrows the channels of our spiritual circulation, putting us at risk.

The plenty that is "too much," as Moore entitles the first section of "The Jerboa," exists in contrast to that "abundance" (section two) which finds its plenty in very little. Self-surrender, or self-denial, may come into it. ("The power of relinquishing / what one would keep; that is freedom," she says in "His Shield.") But under certain circumstances, the soul is governed by the *will to assent* and finds it no struggle to let go of its own projects in deference to the realm of God. This surely is the best of what we know as happiness. Also, as Rumi suggests in one of his own poems, "The Source of Joy," it is what is sometimes meant by poetic inspiration.

> The body turns entirely spirit.
> Leaves become branches in this wind!
>
> Why is it now so easy to surrender,
> Even for those already surrendered?
>
> There's no answer to any of this.
> No one knows the source of joy.
>
> A poet breathes into a reed flute,
> And the tip of every hair makes music. (*Say I Am You*, 20)

As we have seen, much of Elizabeth Bishop's life was a struggle against various kinds of limitation—physical, emotional, economic, and spiritual—and yet two of her greatest poems, "Santarém" and "The Moose," are poems of assent where happiness emerges as an almost ghostly presence capable of feeding the soul and eliminating for a time the burden of suffering meaning.

Where does this ghostly presence come from and, if it is a revenant, how is it connected to the past? In "Anaphora," as you may recall, the "ineffable creature" is spoken of as "assuming memory" and in "The Descent" Williams says: "Memory is a kind of accomplishment, a sort of renewal" and "no whiteness (lost) is so white as the memory of whiteness." In these final pages, I would like to ponder the role that memory plays in this process, both as an obstacle to assent (a painful reminder of better days) and as a faculty that sometimes makes the transcendent accessible. This will take us back to our earlier concern with "time and eternity," while also making it possible for us to see that assent comes as a kind of fulfillment of the promises of other chapters in the life of the spirit, such as the fall, love and longing, suffering meaning, and performing charity.

DIVIDING THE HEART

But first we need to go back to the notion of "suffering meaning," a process that somehow the *wholeness* of assent supersedes. A good way to do this is to think about Elizabeth Bishop's early surrealist poem,

"The Weed" (*CP*, 20–21), which begins in a very "metaphysical" manner reminiscent of the seventeenth-century verse of George Herbert:

> I dreamed that dead, and meditating,
> I lay upon a grave, or bed,
> (at least, some cold and close-built bower).
> In the cold heart, its final thought
> stood frozen, drawn immense and clear,
> stiff and idle as I was there;
> and we remained unchanged together
> for a year, a minute, an hour.
> Suddenly there was a motion
> as startling, there, to every sense
> as an explosion. Then it dropped
> to insistent, cautious creeping
> in the region of the heart,
> prodding me from desperate sleep.
> I raised my head. A slight young weed
> had pushed up through the heart and its
> green head was nodding on the breast.
> (All this was in the dark.)

Bishop readily acknowledged that Herbert's poem "Love Unknown" was in her mind when she wrote "The Weed," and one can certainly see that Herbert's allegory of a heart that is thrown into a font and covered with blood, tossed into a scalding pan to make it supple, and finally pierced by thorns, all in the interests of making it "new, tender," and "quick," has the sort of visceral psychology that Bishop was after in "The Weed." Affliction becomes a blessing in both poems, as the eruption of the alien weed prods Bishop's speaker from the "desperate sleep" in which her thought is frozen.

There is certainly something metaphysical about the operation the speaker's heart undergoes when the weed makes its presence felt.

> The rooted heart began to change
> (not beat) and then it split apart
> and from it broke a flood of water.
> Two rivers glanced off from the sides,
> one to the right, one to the left,
> two rushing, half-clear streams,

reminiscent of the rivers—one coming down the mountain slope and one coming up from underneath—in Milton's *Paradise Lost*. As we hear in a later portion of Bishop's poem, the half-clear streams carry "racing images": "(As if a river should carry all / the scenes that it had once reflected / shut in its waters, and not floating / on momentary surfaces.)"

But what this poem seems to be about is an emotional break-through with implications for both imagistic memory and thought. Bishop was at a low point at the time she wrote this poem, and her allegorizing of paralyzing depression seems on first reading to be far more psychological than spiritual. In the beginning, the dream images are those of death, stasis, and confinement ("some cold and close-built bower"). With its web of roots like nerves ("nervous roots" Bishop calls them) spreading out on each side, the weed inserts itself into the frozen psyche and causes emotional distress, even perhaps tears where Bishop says that the rivers leave their mark as drops on the speaker's face and in her eyes (stippling them, as in "Anaphora"?). One way of understanding the problem that the speaker is having is by relating the scenes locked in the rivers' waters to repressed memories. When she is able to see that "each drop contained a light, / a small, illuminated scene," she is beginning to allow these repressed memories to surface.

However, this poem never gets beyond suffering meaning as an experience of self-division. It never arrives at either spiritual or psychic integration, ending:

> The weed stood in the severed heart.
> "What are you doing there?" I asked.
> It lifted its head all dripping wet
> (with my own thoughts?)
> and answered then: "I grow," it said,
> but to divide your heart again.

The essence of this experience is separation. There may indeed be a metaphysical plot in this poem, but its contours are muted. Unlike Herbert's poem, there is no Master here who might be seen as preparing the heart for grace by these strenuous measures.

A second, more buried, allusion (to Francis Thompson's "The Hound of Heaven") does provide a source for this peculiar weed where, in Thompson, the Divine Pursuer is compared to an "amaranthine weed, / Suffering no flowers except its own to mount." But in "The Hound of Heaven" as in "Love Unknown" the point is to recognize God's hand at work in the world. By contrast, in "The Weed" the machinery of thought is engaged by the liberation of memory

(memory like a weed may return abruptly after it is suppressed), but the mind thinking is a mind forever in motion, making distinctions, dividing up the world. The heart cannot hope for satisfaction, only for renewal, and time is affirmed here, not as a space of plenitude (or eternity) but as an engine of interpretation.

In "The Weed," the experience of change implies violence because there is resistance. Memory must be liberated by some force other than the will, to which the will submits. Assent, by contrast, disarms the force of change, as in Rumi's "The Sign of Being Dried-Up," a poem of assent that can help set the stage for considering Bishop's late poems, "Santarém" and "The Moose." Rumi writes:

> The sign of being a dried-up branch,
> unconnected to root water in the deep ground,
> is that you have no inclination to sway.
>
> Moist, fresh limbs are easily pulled
> any direction, even rounded into
> a hoop for a basket handle.
>
> This is symbolic talk, but the symbol itself
> is a fire to consume your fantasies
> about how you are in union.
>
> Be empty as you go into
> qualities and essence.
>
> Some letters disappear when they elide.
> That way the true meaning emerges.
>
> No words can express how inspired
> words spring out of silence. (*Say I Am You*, 36)

Here memory and all its trappings fall away, as images and fantasies fall away as well. One must let go of everything—"Be empty as you go into / qualities and essence"—and rest in assent. "That way the true meaning emerges," in a poetry that is written *through* the poet as "words spring out of silence."

COMING TOGETHER

Elizabeth Bishop often appears to us as such a highly conscious intellectual that it is hard to locate her at Rumi's well of silence or even at T. S. Eliot's "still point in the turning world." And yet "Santarém" conveys a memory of arrival, silence, and integration that is much closer to Rumi than it is to "The Weed."

The poem concerns a trip Bishop took to the Amazon in 1960, arriving toward evening at the little town of Santarém where two rivers, the Amazon and the Tapajós, come together. She was enchanted, writing to a friend: "I'd like to go there for a rest cure or something—no pavements,—just deep orange sand, beautiful houses and absolute silence" (quoted in Millier, 308). The poem took a long time to write (Bishop didn't finish it until 1978, a year before her death), and what one can see from reading it in various drafts is that the process of integrating her perceptions and letting go of the extraneous material, which was always for her both a psychological and a spiritual process, took a long time.

In the final version, Bishop begins by asserting the unreliability of memory:

> Of course I may be remembering it all wrong
> after, after—how many years?

This, too, ushers in a form of assent. What one has at the end of life is not the world of the remembered experience itself but the imagination of it as it now appears. Can one be satisfied with this alone, with no hope of revision through further contact? Can memory subdue our longings and make us submit to God's will instead of "burning in our minds," as Wallace Stevens put it, "with lost remembrances"? In "Santarém" the answer seems to be yes.

> That golden evening I really wanted to go no further;
> more than anything else I wanted to stay awhile
> in that conflux of two great rivers, Tapajós, Amazon,
> grandly, silently flowing, flowing east.
> Suddenly there'd been houses, people, and lots of mongrel
> riverboats skittering back and forth
> under a sky of gorgeous, under-lit clouds,
> with everything gilded, burnished along one side,
> and everything bright, cheerful, casual—or so it looked.

One should ponder the setting, I think, before going on because the setting is so exuberant, so full of gratitude. It reminds one of Hopkins's poem, "God's Grandeur," that begins: "The world is charged with the grandeur of God" and ends: "Oh, morning, at the brown brink eastward, springs—/ Because the Holy Ghost over the bent / World broods with warm breast and with ah! Bright wings" (38–39). In "Santarém," too, the springs of life are eastward, the clouds are under-lit, the light is golden, the heart with its endless complaints is hushed. No sign of suffering meaning here. Even if this vision is an illusion (as is suggested by "or so it looked"), Bishop assents to it. She lets memory do the work of making the transcendent real, in the process surrendering any attempt either to accurately capture or to control time.

> I liked the place; I liked the idea of the place.
> Two rivers. Hadn't two rivers sprung
> from the Garden of Eden? No, that was four
> and they'd diverged. Here only two
> and coming together. Even if one were tempted
> to literary interpretations
> such as: life/death, right/wrong, male/female
> —such notions would have resolved, dissolved, straight off
> in that watery, dazzling dialectic. (*CP*, 185)

The notion of dialectic is oddly used here and should give us pause. Generally when one speaks of dialectic, one is pointing to the movement of an argument through opposition: thesis opposed by antithesis followed by a synthesis that itself becomes a thesis and thus gives rise once more to a countermove in an endless progression. In the work of Friedrich Hegel, this form of motion provides a paradigm of human history.

Yet, Bishop is speaking of the resolution, and indeed dissolution, of opposites "in that watery, dazzling dialectic." There is something delightfully (perhaps intentionally) paradoxical about this plenitude: a form of transcendence that is held within immanence like a sense of eternity in love with the productions of time. Though the speaker here is not exactly a mystic, the peculiar realm of assent in which this poem dwells renders it, like "At the Fishhouses," approachable through some of the ideas of mysticism.

The work of Michael A. Sells, in *Mystical Languages of Unsaying*, provides some interesting material for this undertaking by focusing our attention on the paradoxical character of mystical writing, as including both *kataphasis* (assertion or speaking with) and *apophasis*, which we encountered in chapter 4 as erasure or unsaying. Apophasis tells us that God, "the source of emanation" to use Sells's language, is no-thing, "not a being or an entity at all." However, language cannot encompass this nothingness. At its best it can only undo its own premises, or, as Sells explains it: "the language of unsaying continually turns back upon the spatial, temporal, and ontological reifications it has posed" (208).

One of the principal tensions in mysticism is between transcendence and immanence. Though it is commonly believed that mysticism is all about transcendence, in fact Sells argues that in apophasis, "the hierarchical levels of being that are [thus] posited are unsaid from within. At the heart of unsaying is a radical *dialectic* of transcendence and immanence. That which is utterly 'beyond' is revealed or reveals itself as most intimately 'within': within the 'just act' however humble . . . , within the basic acts of perception . . . , within the act of interpreting . . . , or within the act of love" (7).

As we have seen, these four concerns—the just act, the basic acts of perception, the act of interpreting, and the act of love—could be used to map the four principle directions of Bishop's poetry. We have also used them here to consider four aspects of the Christian life: practicing charity, perceiving eternity inside time, suffering meaning, and experiencing human love as a longing for God. I want to suggest that we can see all of these moves—as well as their opposites—in the "watery, dazzling dialectic" of "Santarém."

Yet the appeal that this poem makes is to common experience. How many of us have *not* experienced in some beautiful outdoor setting this worshipful wonder? The details of this milieu are thoroughly specific, recognizable, even while being exotic.

> In front of the church, the Cathedral, rather,
> there was a modest promenade and a belvedere
> about to fall into the river,
> stubby palms, flamboyants like pans of embers,
> buildings one story high, stucco, blue or yellow,
> and one house faced with *azulejos*, buttercup yellow.
> The street was deep in dark gold river sand
> damp from the ritual afternoon rain,
> and teams of zebus plodded, gentle, proud,
> and *blue*, with down-curved horns and hanging ears,
> pulling carts with solid wheels.
> The zebus' hooves, the people's feet
> waded in golden sand,
> dampered by golden sand,
> so that almost the only sounds
> were creaks and *shush, shush, shush*.

Transcendence and immanence are here wedded. Anaphora, in the form of many echoes such as "waded in golden sand / dampered by golden sand," reinforces the sense that the Creation is full of repetitions, interpretable in terms of both divergence and convergence, but the shush / shush / shush sounds at the end of this stanza (like the so-so-so of "Filling Station") suggest the soothing of the heart's murmurings that mysteriously accompanies the feeling of assent, simultaneously a psychological and a spiritual experience.

In line with the wedding of immanence and transcendence, a metaphor of intercourse subtends the long central stanza where the two rivers come together: "Two rivers full of crazy shipping— people / all apparently changing their minds, embarking / disembarking, rowing clumsy dories." Southern families who moved there with their slaves have left blue eyes among the populace. A dozen or so young nuns are waving gaily as they head "up God knows what lost tributary" to assume their mission. And a cow balances, "quite calm," in a wobbling dugout carrying her off "to be married." "Intercourse" is of varying kinds here: spatial, commercial, social (waving), sexual, and spiritual. Where a river schooner with its masts raked for speed seems on the verge of touching the church "(Cathedral, rather!)," time and eternity cross.

Everything envisioned is, in fact, touched by the paradoxical splendor of the miraculous. Even a wasps' nest, much admired by the speaker—"small, exquisite, clean matte white, / and hard as stucco"— seems a miracle of construction and preservation, so that when the pharmacist responds to this admiration by giving her the nest, that too seems part and parcel of this miraculous place.

But of course if this is really going to be a poem of saying and unsaying, we have to see in it a countermovement "turning back upon the spatial, temporal, ontological reifications it has posed," as Sells says. Thus, we have instances of simultaneous inflation and deflation, epitomized by the repetition of "church," followed by "Cathedral, rather!" which, strangely, seems to deflate it by deliberately overstating its case. The miraculous aspects of the scene are lightly and humorously deflated by a local story of miraculous preservation.

> A week or so before
> there'd been a thunderstorm and the Cathedral'd
> been struck by lightning. One tower had
> a widening zigzag crack all the way down.
> It was a miracle. The priest's house right next door
> had been struck, too, and his brass bed
> (the only one in town) galvanized black.
> *Graças a deus*—he'd been in Belém. (*CP*, 186)

From a "modern" point of view, the miracle is not really a miracle, merely a strange phenomenon, but the brass bed, "galvanized black," when looked at from a surrealist point of view, might well be miraculous after all. Similarly, in terms of performing charity (the just act), there is also a countermove: the charitable pharmacist, who spontaneously gives, shares the stage with the slave owners who ignominiously take. As for perception, eternity captured in the exotic details ("gorgeous, under-lit clouds," for example), is unsaid from within where the poet announces that she may be remembering it "all wrong." Even the act of interpretation (what we have called "suffering meaning") is presented through both kataphasis (saying) and apophasis (unsaying): every thing is bright, cheerful, casual, "or so it looked."

Ultimately, the mystical language of paradox and parallax, which Sells describes as typically present in water-sun-fire (here river-light-embers) imagery, affirms both the sense of transcendent synchrony and its opposite, disparity, in the radical immanence of dissent and departure with which the poem ends.

> In the blue pharmacy the pharmacist
> had hung an empty wasps' nest from a shelf:
> small, exquisite, clean matte white,
> and hard as stucco. I admired it
> so much he gave it to me.
> Then—my ship's whistle blew. I couldn't stay.
> Back on board, a fellow passenger, Mr. Swan,
> Dutch, the retiring head of Phillips Electric,
> really a very nice old man,
> who wanted to see the Amazon before he died,
> asked "What's that ugly thing?" (*CP*, 186–87)

Bishop and Mr. Swan see the world from very different points of view, an example of what Sells calls "parallax." And as we move into difference again, we find once more that nothing gold can stay. It's like the end of "At the Fishhouses" where the epiphany must assent to its own dissolution, emptying itself into history, which is "flowing, and flown." The central feature of assent, which is relinquishing the desire for control over time, presents itself here as an acceptance of the loss implied in moving on.

There is, of course, no acknowledgment of God in this poem. There are lots of allusions to religion—the Garden of Eden, the church (Cathedral, rather), nuns, the priest, a miracle—but this poem, like most of Bishop's poems, is not overtly devotional. Unless, of course, one sees that it is all about the realm of God. Its title—though it does refer to an actual place named Santarém in Brazil—evokes a Latinate hint of "sacred things."

OTHERWORLDLINESS

Why do some places, people, and experiences, though strange or exotic, seem so familiar? Or conversely, how does a sense of other-worldliness emerge in the usually prosaic present, as it did, clearly, for Elizabeth Bishop in Santarém? William Wordsworth thought that such a sense might be explained by the fact that we have inherent in us a memory of "elsewhere." In his "Ode: Intimations of Immortality," Wordsworth famously wrote:

> Our birth is but a sleep and a forgetting:
> The Soul that rises with us, our life's Star,
>   Hath had elsewhere its setting,
>   And cometh from afar:
>   Not in entire forgetfulness,
>   And not in utter nakedness,
> But trailing clouds of glory do we come
> From God who is our home. (154)

This conception helps us to see how memory might be related to assent. If we still have a rudimentary memory of our prehistory, its reawakening might give us the courage to let go of our will.

Wordsworth thought that this kind of memory was dulled as we grew older: "Shades of the prison-house begin to close / Upon the growing boy." But Elizabeth Bishop, who once called herself "something of a minor Wordsworth," clearly knew moments of echo and return that might have made her chime in with the Romantic poet where he breaks out: "O joy! That in our embers / Is something that doth live, / That nature yet remembers / What was so fugitive!" (156). These are moments of exultation and assent that can at least temporarily cancel our feelings of alienation and exile. Perhaps Bishop's "pan of embers" in "Santarém" is intended to remind us of Wordsworth's joy.

"The Moose" is another poem that chronicles this kind of experience. It is also one of Bishop's best and most lovable works, containing memorable descriptions of a bus ride through eastern Canada as well as examples of Bishop's characteristic humor. It took her over twenty-five years to get the poem into final form. Though it recounts an experience she had in 1946, she did not finish it until she had to present it at a Phi Beta Kappa ceremony in 1972, and its ultimate aspect of serenity distinguishes it in some ways from the other poem she wrote about this trip, "At the Fishhouses," which was completed earlier. Whereas the latter poem is an affecting example of "suffering meaning," "The Moose" shares with some of Bishop's other late poems, such as "Santarém," "The End of March," and "Sonnet," the sense of being surprised by joy.

James Merrill commented that Bishop's late poems demonstrate both acceptance and serenity, but Bishop herself felt that what connects poems like "Poem" and "The Moose" is that both concern "life and the memory of it so compressed / they've turned into each other" ("Poem," *CP*, 177). She wrote to John Frederick Nims that "The Moose" was mostly about "childhood recollections" (*One Art*, 638), an odd comment (since it seems *mostly* about an experience she had as an adult) and yet it helps us to understand how this poem is geared to the operations of memory.

"The Moose" begins with a series of evocative stanzas about a bus trip through Nova Scotia and New Brunswick, alluding to the Bay of Fundy—"where the bay leaves the sea/ twice a day and takes / the herrings long rides." The Bay of Fundy has the highest tides in the world, as much as fifty feet of water changing places in the tidal shift:

> Where, silted red,
> sometimes the sun sets
> facing a red sea,
> and others, veins the flats'
> lavender, rich mud
> in burning rivulets. (*CP*, 169)

Bishop took this bus trip from Great Village to Boston, after visiting her favorite aunt, Grace Bulmer Bowers, to whom the poem is dedicated. She describes herself as "a lone traveler" saying goodbye to seven relatives before boarding the bus, while "a collie supervises." In the first long section of the poem, the poet suggests a contrast between the ghostly, almost hallucinatory landscape outside the bus window and the people inside, one of whom is herself, jauntily setting off all alone for the long trip to Massachusetts.

> Goodbye to the elms,
> to the farm, to the dog.
> The bus starts. The light
> grows richer; the fog,
> shifting, salty thin,
> comes closing in.
>
> Its cold, round crystals
> form and slide and settle
> in the white hens' feathers,

> in gray glazed cabbages,
> on the cabbage roses
> and lupins like apostles.
>
> The sweet peas cling
> to their wet white string
> on the whitewashed fences;
> bumblebees creep
> inside the foxgloves,
> and evening commences. (170)

Mostly she is describing a familiar, much loved landscape here. There is only one simile—"lupins like apostles"—standing upright in the middle of this description and making us think of witnesses, but witnesses to what? Just as the upright lupins might be seen as figures of courage, so the grandmotherly figure who clambers aboard the bus a little later—"brisk, freckled, elderly," a recollection of Bishop's own grandmother, perhaps—has that aura of inner strength required of assent. She speaks to the bus driver: "A grand night. Yes, sir, / all the way to Boston. / She regards us amicably."

But now, "as we enter / the New Brunswick woods," the poem takes on a different tone, the moonlight and mist seeming to enter the bus itself, almost as though putting the passengers under a spell or into a Romantic revery.

> The passengers lie back.
> Snores. Some long sighs.
> A dreamy divagation
> begins in the night,
> a gentle, auditory,
> slow hallucination . . . .
>
> In the creakings and noises,
> an old conversation
> —not concerning us,
> but recognizable, somewhere,
> back in the bus:
> Grandparents' voices
>
> uninterruptedly
> talking, in Eternity: (CP, 171)

Many readers have noted that this vision of the grandparents talking in eternity is not just a vision of anyone's grandparents but specifically of Bishop's own. Bonnie Costello writes: "These are her own grandparents she remembers, talking of people in her family or village, though now their overheard conversation is projected into a domestic concept of 'Eternity.' 'Eternity' for Bishop is the end of the line, a retrospective rather than a transcendent point of view in which anxiety, regret, anticipation have no place. It is not a place of mastery . . . but of acceptance" (165).

Several of the stories now mentioned in the poem have specific relevance to Bishop's family: "the son lost / when the schooner foundered" (Robert Hutchinson, Bishop's great grandfather); the one who "took to drink" (her uncle Arthur or perhaps herself), and then the passage discussed earlier with reference to Bishop's mother: "When Amos began to pray / even in the store and / finally the family had / to put him away." If "Amos" is a pseudonym for Gertrude Bulmer Bishop, her religious fanaticism no longer has the power to make Bishop herself fearful. It is followed here by a passage directly on assent.

> "Yes . . ." that peculiar
> affirmative. "Yes . . ."
> A sharp, indrawn breath,
> half groan, half acceptance,
> that means "Life's like that.
> We know *it* (also death)."

Memory converges with acceptance here, as the grandparents are imagined speaking to one another in Eternity and the memory of her own grandparents generates a sense of security that allows reconciliation with the past.

> Talking the way they talked
> in the old featherbed,
> peacefully, on and on,
> dim lamplight in the hall,
> down in the kitchen, the dog
> tucked in her shawl.

The dog is reminiscent of "Filling Station" 's dirty dog on the wicker sofa, "quite comfy." It is part of that same intuition that "somebody loves us all," a sense that also introduces the next lines in "The Moose": "Now, it is all right now / even to fall asleep / just as on all those nights." She is letting go under the spell of a benign maternal presence (now, now), the two "now"s alerting us to the way certain kinds of memory allow us to surrender to the present, "just as on all those nights." This is the wisdom of assent, which, in its religious character, implies an accommodation, a surrender like my friend Pam's, to God's will.

Thus, it is not entirely surprising that this busload of seemingly assenting individuals is suddenly blessed with an epiphanic appearance. Right in the middle of the stanza about feeling able to let go of anxiety and fall asleep, Bishop startles us:

> —Suddenly the bus driver
> stops with a jolt,
> turns off his lights.
>
> A moose has come out of
> the impenetrable wood
> and stands there, looms, rather,
> in the middle of the road.
> It approaches; it sniffs at
> the bus's hot hood.
>
> Towering, antlerless,
> high as a church,
> homely as a house
> (or, safe as houses). (*CP*, 172–73)

Just as in "Santarém," transcendence ("high as a church") converges with immanence: "homely as a house." Bishop treats us to some of the hushed, prosaic comments of the other passengers, whom she describes in Wordsworthian terms as feeling strangely "childish" in the presence of this odd creature: "Perfectly harmless . . ." "It's awful plain," "Look! It's a she!" One might speak of the moose as a ghostly revenant, the destructive mother now returning as a benign emissary.

> Taking her time,
> she looks the bus over,
> grand, otherworldly.
> Why, why do we feel
> (we all feel) this sweet
> sensation of joy?

It's almost Wordsworthian. "Oh joy! That in our embers / Is something that doth live, / That nature yet remembers / What was so fugitive." The experience of the otherworldly here gives these individuals a sense of oneness: "we *all* feel." Joy feeds assent and assent makes room for the experience of joy. Even if such feelings

do not last, they leave a trace of something (something pungent)
behind:

> by craning backward,
> the moose can be seen
> on the moonlit macadam;
> then there's a dim
> smell of moose, an acrid
> smell of gasoline. (*CP*, 173)

GOOD TO EAT A THOUSAND YEARS

In Allen Ginsberg's ecstatic religious paean to the Beat Movement,
"Howl" (1956), he speaks of himself and his friends as attempting to
"set the noun and dash of consciousness together jumping with
sensation of Pater Omnipotens Aeterna Deus," "putting down
here what might be left to say in time come after death," bringing to
us, at the end of section one, "the absolute heart of the poem of
life butchered out of their own bodies good to eat a thousand
years" (16).

The San Francisco Poetry Movement did not really appeal to
Elizabeth Bishop, even though she lived in its environs for more than
a year. But she too was caught up, especially in her late poetry, with
the attempt to create a profound affirmation of life that would speak
in the registers of both time and eternity. And her poetry still has
something to say to us about the spiritual issues she thought
significant: in addition to time and eternity, these are the fall, love
and longing, suffering meaning, charity, and assent. In a poem
Elizabeth Bishop admired, William Carlos Williams wrote: "It is difficult / to get the news from poems / yet men die miserably every day
for lack / of what is found there" ("Asphodel, That Greeny Flower,"
161–62).

We must take time with poetry and no summary can do it justice.
But in the aftermath of thinking about Bishop's treatment of assent,
it may not be amiss to reflect upon where we have been in this series
of meditations about poems and religious meanings. In terms of
"the fall," Bishop's poem "The Prodigal" helps us to see in concrete
terms the distortion of perspective and sense of isolation that follow
from self-destructive behavior, as "Roosters" reminds us that an
important part of the consciousness of sin is forgiveness, including
self-forgiveness. " 'Deny deny deny' / is not all the roosters cry."
Part of accepting God's will (in "Roosters") involves reading the

wandering lines of scripture in the always renewable resources of
creation:

> In the morning
> a low light is floating
> in the backyard, and gilding
>
> from underneath
> the broccoli, leaf by leaf;
> how could the night have come to grief?
>
> gilding the tiny
> floating swallow's belly
> and lines of pink cloud in the sky,
>
> the days' preamble
> like wandering lines in marble. (*CP*, 39)

In "Love and Longing" (chapter 3), we encountered those wandering lines again in Bishop's poem on the Bible, "Over 2,000
Illustrations and a Complete Concordance," where "the lines that
move apart / like ripples above sand" are called "God's spreading
fingerprint." Just as her description of the operations of love in
"Filling Station" brings us into the realm of God, where "Somebody
loves us all," so dissatisfaction (*lack of* assent) in the Bible poem
reveals our longing for meaning as a longing for the feeling of God's
presence: "Why couldn't we have seen / this old Nativity while we
were at it?" There is no real faith without this dark night of the soul,
this feeling of loss and longing.

But thinking about love also means thinking about comedy: the
"gray crochet" of the doily in the dirty filling station and the dog on
the wicker sofa, "quite comfy." Even in "Over 2,000 Illustrations" the
Nativity scene rendered as "a family with pets" is comic in its way.
And William F. Lynch's comments about the "limited concrete" as
the path to insight and salvation, what he calls "an art of anamnesis,
or memory, of the bloody human (in the sense in which the English
use that adjective) as a path to God, or to any form of the great"
(104), help us to see how comedy can be a form of love that is
premised upon assent. Not always. But sometimes, as in that "sweet
sensation of joy" in "The Moose." The moose herself, in being larger
than life, is ungainly, a wonderfully comic form of the divine.

In chapter 4 we considered "suffering meaning" as both a tragic
and a comic experience. Premised on a perception of difference and
separation, the place Emily Dickinson depicts as "where the meanings
are" may sometimes also bring to mind the experience of God's

absence, as it does in "Over 2,000 Illustrations" and in poems of spiritual affliction by Gerard Manley Hopkins and George Herbert. The Dark Night of the Soul is a time when suffering *becomes* meaningful because we experience our sense of being as a painful limitation: Elizabeth Bishop's horror of "*I, I, I*" and Gerard Manley Hopkins's taste of himself as gall and heartburn.

But even in the midst of this, God sometimes surprises earth with heaven, as in "The End of March" when there is the sun again, a sun "who perhaps had batted a kite out of the sky to play with." He reminds us of the comedy of life and of the totality of which we are a part. The seal in Bishop's "At the Fishhouses" is a comedian, "like me a believer in total immersion." But even if we cannot bear the full weight of knowledge, we can feel its edge as suffering and assent to it in the way of those elders speaking in the back of the bus in "The Moose": "Life's like that. / We know *it* (also death)."

That totality of which we are a part is more centrally the subject of chapter 5—"Blessed Are the Poor"—and of poems such as "In the Waiting Room," "Squatter's Children," "Manuelzinho," and "Pink Dog." The essence of true charity seems to be its lack of connection to calculations of profit or risk. Its higher connection here is to something we should call Justice. In God's order, it is just to care for those in need because we are all parts of the Creation and stewards of what is ultimately not our own. Mamie Harris in Bishop's "Mercedes Hospital" is a saint because she is unselfconscious about practicing charity. She does it for no ulterior reason, simply bringing relief to all her patients, even those who do not necessarily deserve it. Her form of assent is expressed in her willingness to be used up in this process.

Does all this mean that we are compelled to be passive, to assent rather than dissent, in the face of injustice? "Pink Dog," a powerful expression of political feeling, says no. Bishop was not a saint, but she intervened where she could to help others, especially the poor. More importantly, she was a writer, and she used her writing to raise important questions about who we are and where we can find meaning. Though our grasp of it is necessarily intermittent, one should keep in mind her image of the poet as a marksman: "The target is a moving target, and the marksman is also moving." We should also remember the passage she copied out from Kierkegaard: "Poetry is illusion before knowledge; religion illusion after knowledge. Between poetry and religion the worldly wisdom of living plays its comedy. Every individual who does not live either poetically or religiously [or both] is a fool."

It hardly needs restating that Elizabeth Bishop was not a Christian, but as Richard Wilbur rightly put it, "she had many

Christian associations [from her upbringing], cared about many Christian things, and had got [them] into her poems here and there . . . that's what she was left with, the questions, if not the answers, of a person with a religious temperament" (Fountain and Brazeau, 349). She lived poetically, and in a sense religiously, and thus was not, at least according to Kierkegaard, a fool.

We must also recognize that poems have a way of getting away from their writers and sometimes they get into deeper water than the poet realizes. That certainly seems to be the case with Bishop, who could write a poem called "A Miracle for Breakfast" without realizing (until it was pointed out to her) that some might be inclined to think of the Eucharist. As long as we are conscientious about language, we are free to make of poems what we will. If they are meaningful to some of us for reasons she did not intend, Bishop would have been the last one to cavil. The world of poetry, as she saw it, was endlessly reinterpretable, forever open to new opportunities for seeing further and seeing more. In a poetic fragment entitled "Walk Around Here & Now" she suggests that the world of Creation is always open to the curious and the worshipful:

> After the rain the puddles are blue.
> As St. Theresa said of God:
> "There are little pools for children,
> there are pools for all,
> some large, some small." (KWN, Vassar Archive)*

---

* This poem was published in *The New Yorker* (December 23, 2002) under the title "After the Rain" with the word "grace" instead of "God." However, the word is smeared in both the Key West Notebook and Bishop's 1940s fair copy ("After the Rain"). In my opinion, there is no justification for choosing the word "grace" over "God." Bishop is quoting Teresa's *Way of Perfection*, chapter 20, where she says that the Lord has different roads by which people may come to him. He does not force any to drink from his fountain of life. "For from this rich spring flow many streams—some large, others small, and also little pools for children, which they find quite large enough, for the sight of a great deal of water [of God, not grace] would frighten them: by children, I mean those who are in the early stages" of religious pursuit (146). It's obvious that Teresa is speaking not of grace but of God here. Bishop was extremely precise about attributions and criticized those who were not.

WORKS CITED

UNPUBLISHED SOURCES

Final Exam for English 285 (January 27, 1973). Elizabeth Bishop Collection. Vassar College Library.

Key West Notebook of Elizabeth Bishop in Elizabeth Bishop Collection. Vassar College Library. Poughkeepsie, New York.

Unpublished correspondence with Robert Lowell. Elizabeth Bishop Collection. Vassar College Library.

Unpublished correspondence with Anne Stevenson. Special Collections. Washington University in St. Louis. St. Louis, Mo.

Unpublished correspondence with Joseph and U. T. Summers. Elizabeth Bishop Collection. Vassar College Library.

PUBLISHED SOURCES

Augustine. *The City of God*. Trans. Gerald Walsh, Demetrius Zema, and Grace Monahan. Ed. Vernon J. Bourke. Garden City, N.Y.: Image Books, 1958.

Bible. *The New Scofield Study Bible*. King James Version. Ed. C. I. Scofield. Nashville: Thomas Nelson, 1989.

Bishop, Elizabeth. *The Collected Prose*. New York: Farrar, Straus, 1984.

———. *The Complete Poems: 1927–1979*. New York: Farrar, Straus, 1983.

———. *One Art*. Ed. Robert Giroux. New York: Farrar, Straus, 1994.

———. "Seven Christian Hymns." *Poetry Pilot* (October 1964): 14–20.

Buechner, Frederick. *The Longing for Home*. New York: HarperSanFrancisco, 1996.

Carlson, Thomas A. "The Poverty and Poetry of Indiscretion: Negative Theology and Negative Anthropology in Contemporary and Historical Perspective." *Christianity and Literature* 47 (1998): 167–94.

The Cloud of Unknowing and the Book of Privy Counseling. Ed. William Johnston. New York: Doubleday-Image Books, 1973.

Colwell, Anne. *Inscrutable Houses: Metaphors of the Body in the Poems of Elizabeth Bishop*. Tuscaloosa: University of Alabama Press, 1997.

Costello, Bonnie. *Elizabeth Bishop: Questions of Mastery*. Cambridge: Harvard University Press, 1991.

Dargan, Joan. *Simone Weil: Thinking Poetically*. Albany: SUNY Press, 1999.

Detweiler, Robert. *Breaking the Fall: Religious Readings of Contemporary Fiction*. London: Macmillan, 1989.

Dickie, Margaret. *Stein, Bishop, & Rich: Lyrics of Love, War, & Place*. Chapel Hill: University of North Carolina Press, 1997.

Dickinson, Emily. *The Poems of Emily Dickinson*. Variorum Edition. 3 vols. Ed. Thomas H. Johnson. Cambridge: Harvard University Press, 1955.

Eliot, T. S. *Collected Poems 1909–1962*. New York: Harcourt Brace, 1963.

Fitzgerald, Constance. "Desolation as Dark Night: The Transformative Influence of Wisdom in John of the Cross." *The Way* (Supplement) 82 (Spring 1995): 96–108.

Fountain, Gary and Peter Brazeau. *Elizabeth Bishop: An Oral Biography*. Amherst: University of Massachusetts Press, 1994.

Ginsberg, Allen. *Howl and Other Poems*. San Francisco: City Lights Books, 1959.

Habermas, Jurgen. "Modernity versus Postmodernity." Trans. Seila Ben-Habib. *New German Critique* 22 (1981): 3–14.

Hamilton, Jane. *A Map of the World*. New York: Doubleday, 1994.

Hawthorne, Nathaniel. *Selected Tales and Sketches*. New York: Penguin Books, 1987.

Heaney, Seamus. *The Government of the Tongue*. New York: Farrar, Straus, 1989.

Henry, Patrick. *The Ironic Christian's Companion*. New York: Riverhead Books, 1999.

Herbert, George. *The Complete English Poems*. New York: Penguin Books, 1991.

Hill, Geoffrey. *For the Unfallen: Poems 1952–58*. London: Deutsch, 1959.

Hopkins, Gerard Manley. *Immortal Diamond: The Spiritual Vision of Gerard Manley Hopkins*. New York: Doubleday-Image Books, 1995.

Huxley, Aldous. *The Perennial Philosophy*. London: Fontana Books, 1958.

Ignatius of Loyola. *Spiritual Exercises*. Ed. Rev. C. Lattey. St. Louis: Herder, 1928.

Impasto, David. *Upholding Mystery: An Anthology of Contemporary Christian Poetry*. New York: Oxford University Press, 1997.

Jarraway, David. *Wallace Stevens and the Question of Belief: Metaphysician in the Dark*. Baton Rouge: Louisiana State University Press, 1993.

John of the Cross. *The Dark Night of the Soul*. Ed. Halcyon Backhouse. London: Hodder and Stoughton, 1988.

Lombardi, Marilyn May. *Elizabeth Bishop: The Geography of Gender*. Charlottesville: University Press of Virginia, 1993.

Lowell, Robert. *Lord Weary's Castle and the Mills of the Kavanaughs*. New York: Harcourt Brace, 1961.

Lynch, William F., S.J. *Christ and Apollo: The Dimensions of the Literary Imagination*. New York: Sheed and Ward, 1960.

McCabe, Susan. *Elizabeth Bishop: Her Poetics of Loss*. University Park: Pennsylvania State University Press, 1994.

McClatchy, J. D. *White Paper: On Contemporary American Poetry*. New York: Columbia University Press, 1989.

Merrin, Jeredith. *An Enabling Humility: Marianne Moore, Elizabeth Bishop, and the Uses of Tradition*. New Brunswick: Rutgers University Press, 1990.

Millay, Edna St. Vincent. "Into the golden vessel of great song," in *Collected Poems*. New York: Harper & Row, 1956, p. 573.

Millier, Brett. *Elizabeth Bishop: Life and the Memory of It*. Berkeley: University of California Press, 1993.

Milton, John. *Paradise Lost*. Ed. Merritt Y. Hughes. Upper Saddle River, N.J.: Prentice-Hall, 1997.

Monteiro, George. *Conversations with Elizabeth Bishop*. Jackson: University Press of Mississippi, 1996.

Moore, Marianne. *The Complete Poems of Marianne Moore*. New York: Macmillan, 1967.

O'Connor, Flannery. *Everything that Rises Must Converge*. New York: Farrar, Straus, 1965.

Rilke, Rainer Maria. *Duino Elegies*. Trans. Stephen Mitchell. Boston: Shambhala, 1992.

Rimbaud, Arthur. *Complete Works, Selected Letters*. Trans. Wallace Fowlie. Chicago: University of Chicago Press, 1966.

Roman, Camille. *Elizabeth Bishop's World War II—Cold War View*. New York: Palgrave-Macmillan, 2001.

Rotella, Guy. *Reading & Writing Nature*. Boston: Northeastern University Press, 1991.

Rumi, Jalal-uddin. *The Essential Rumi*. Trans. Coleman Barks with John Moyne, A. J. Arberry, and Reynold Nicholson. New York: HarperSanFrancisco, 1995.

———. *Open Secret*. Trans. John Moyne and Coleman Barks. Putney, Vt.: Threshold Books, 1984.

———. *Say I Am You*. Trans. John Moyne and Coleman Barks. Athens, Ga.: Maypop Books, 1994.

Schwartz, Lloyd and Sybil P. Estess. *Elizabeth Bishop and Her Art*. Ann Arbor: University of Michigan Press, 1983.

Sells, Michael A. *Mystical Languages of Unsaying*. Chicago: University of Chicago Press, 1994.

Shore, Jane. "Elizabeth Bishop: The Art of Changing Your Mind." *Ploughshares* 5 (1979): 178–91.

Stevens, Wallace. *The Palm at the End of the Mind: Selected Poems and a Play*. Ed. Holly Stevens. New York: Knopf, 1971.

Stevenson, Anne. *Between the Iceberg and the Ship*. Ann Arbor: University of Michigan Press, 1998.

———. *Elizabeth Bishop*. New York: Twayne, 1966.

Teresa of Avila. *The Collected Works of St. Teresa of Avila*. 3 vols. Trans. Kieran Kavanaugh and Otilio Rodriguez. Washington, D.C.: ICS Publications, 1987.

Teresa of Avila. *The Way of Perfection.* Trans. E. Allison Peers. New York: Doubleday-Image, 1991.

Thompson, Francis. "The Hound of Heaven" in *Century Readings for a Course in English Literature.* Ed. J. W. Cunliffe. New York: Century Company, 1924.

Travisano, Thomas. *Elizabeth Bishop: Her Artistic Development.* Charlottesville: University Press of Virginia, 1988.

Warren, Robert Penn and Albert Erskine, eds. *Six Centuries of Great Poetry.* New York: Dell Publishing Co., 1955.

Weil, Simone. *Waiting for God.* Trans. Emma Crauford. New York: Harper & Row, 1973.

Williams, William Carlos. *Pictures from Breughel and Other Poems.* London: MacGibbon & Kee, 1963.

Winterson, Jeanette. "The Queen of Spades" in *The Passion* in *Venice.* Ed. John and Kirsten Miller. San Francisco: Chronicle Books, 1994.

Wordsworth, William. *The Prelude, Selected Poems and Sonnets.* Ed. Carlos Baker. New York: Holt Rinehart, 1954.

Wyschogrod, Michael. "Martin Buber" in *The Encyclopedia of Philosophy,* Vol. 1. New York: Macmillan, 1967.

About the Author

Cheryl Walker is Richard Armour Professor of Modern Languages at Scripps College. Her books on American women poets (*The Nightingale's Burden* and *Masks Outrageous and Austere*) have been widely influential. In 1997 she published *Indian Nation: Native American Literature and Nineteenth-Century Nationalisms*. Walker teaches in several programs at Scripps, including English and Religious Studies, and is a member of the United Church of Christ, Congregational, in Claremont, California.

INDEX